THE EARTH BOOK

First published in 2015 by
Miles Kelly Publishing Ltd
Harding's Barn, Bardfield End Green,
Thaxted, Essex, CM6 3PX, UK

This edition published 2021

10 9 8 7 6 5 4 3 2 1

Publishing Director Belinda Gallagher
Creative Director Jo Cowan
Managing Editor Amanda Askew
Managing Designer Simon Lee

Senior Editors Rosie Neave, Carly Blake,
Claire Philip
Assistant Editors Amy Johnson, Lauren White
Designers Simon Lee (cover), D&A Design,
Rocket Design
Proofreaders Carly Blake, Fran Bromage
Image Manager Liberty Newton
Production Controller Jennifer Brunwin
Reprographics Stephan Davis
Assets Lorraine King

ISBN 978-1-78989-424-0

Printed in China

British Library Cataloging-in-Publication Data
A catalog record for this book is available
from the British Library

Made with paper from a sustainable forest

www.mileskelly.net

THE EARTH

Contributors

Camilla de la Bédoyère

Steve Parker

John Farndon

Miles Kelly

BOOK

Contents

Active Earth **6-41**

Vast Oceans **42-77**

Earth's Wonders **78–113**

Earth's Power **114–149**

Index **150**

Acknowledgments **158**

Active EARTH

Our planet is at the mercy of awesome natural forces. Even beneath its rocky surface, Earth is constantly on the move.

Visitors from Space	8
Cracking Up	10
Mightiest Mountain	12
Ultimate Volcano	14
Hot Spots	16
Crunch Time	18
Greatest River	20
Extreme Erosion	22
Freezing Flow	24
Enter the Abyss	26
Buried Treasure	28
Deep-sea Dive	30
Wild Winds	32
Freaky Weather	34
Ultra Freeze	36
The Ends of the Earth	38
Super Dry	40

◀ The pattern of lines in this rock face in the Paria Canyon-Vermilion Cliffs Wilderness, on the border of Utah and Arizona, U.S., is caused by layers of compressed sandstone worn smooth by glacier erosion.

Visitors from
SPACE

Our planet is a **boiling**, heaving, freezing, **dynamic place** to live. Mud bubbles, winds whip **the** air into spinning spirals, and vast **cracks** open in the ground. Our extreme Earth **formed** 4.6 billion years ago, but visitors from space constantly remind us of our **place** in a bigger, even more extreme, **Universe.**

Fireballs

Meteoroids are lumps of rock or metallic stone that burn with a fierce heat when entering Earth's atmosphere. Their glowing trails of gases and melted particles are called meteor showers, shooting stars, or fireballs. The most brilliant meteor shower occurred in the U.S. in 1883. As thousands of glittering lights fell through the sky, people woke from their sleep, fearing the end of the world.

Total wipeout!

The cataclysmic K-P Event occurred 65.5 million years ago. The impact of a meteorite crash near Chicxulub, Mexico, threw dust and rock into the air, blocking sunlight and affecting the climate for 10,000 years. Scientists believe this caused the extinction of about 80 percent of animal species, including dinosaurs.

If another giant meteorite heads toward Earth, it could raise the temperature of the air beneath it to 100,000°F (about 60,000°C)—ten times hotter than the Sun's surface. The impact could blast 250 cu mi (about 1,000 cu km) of rock and gas into the air, and produce shock waves that trigger earthquakes.

Polar light show

Some of Earth's most staggering sights are the aurorae, when night skies around the North and South poles are lit up by ghostly curtains of light that sweep across the darkness. This extreme effect is caused by the action of Earth's magnetic field on streams of particles that have been carried from the Sun on a solar wind.

▲ *Aurora australis* (Southern Lights), seen from the International Space Station (ISS).

THE LARGEST METEORITE CRATER IS AT VREDEFORT IN SOUTH AFRICA. IT HAS A DIAMETER OF 180 MI (ABOUT 300 KM).

▼ Comet Hyakutake, seen on March 21, 1996.

Burning ice

Comets are chunks of ice, rock, and frozen gases that become superheated as they near the Sun, and produce flares of bright light. In 1996 the path of the comet Hyakutake took it close to Earth—a mere 9 million mi (15 million km) away—and it became one of the brightest celestial events for 200 years. The comet is now heading toward the edges of the Solar System and won't be seen again for 72,000 years.

▲ U.S. astronaut James Irwin described Earth from space as "a sparkling blue-and-white jewel."

CRACKING Up

At Earth's center, **temperatures** reach a staggering 9,800°F (about 5,400°C). Like a mighty engine room, this **hot core** powers vast movements of rock and causes the planet's outer crust to break into **sections** and move. The result is an **array** of awesome seismic events, from the creation of **mountains** to earthquakes in all **their** destructive power.

TECTONIC PLATES

North American Plate

Eurasian Plate

Philippine Plate

Australian Plate

Solid inner core made from iron and nickel

Liquid outer core

Heat from the core passes through the almost-solid lower mantle

Material in the upper mantle can flow slightly

Pressure from the mantle can cause the rocky crust to crack

▲ Inside Earth, there are layers of different material, heated by the core.

The Pacific Ring of Fire

Thanks to its fearsome history, the world's most violent area of seismic activity is known as the Pacific Ring of Fire. With more than 75 percent of the world's volcanoes and active plate movements, this region is responsible for much of the planet's geology, including the Andes, Mount St. Helens, the islands of Japan, and Krakatau, one of the planet's most explosive volcanoes.

◀ Volcanic steam escapes from a vent in Antarctica.

A growing ocean

The Atlantic Ocean conceals the world's longest mountain chain—the Mid-Atlantic Ridge. These massive underwater peaks create a ridge 10,000 mi (about 16,000 km) in length, where plates meet over a hot region of mantle. Lava adds to the crust, building up the plates and forcing them further apart.

▶ Cracks and tears appear in Iceland, following the line of the Mid-Atlantic Ridge.

Eurasian Plate

Arabian Plate

African Plate

Indian Plate

South American Plate

Nazca Plate

◀ In 2010, Iceland's Eyjafjallajökull volcano wreaked travel havoc when it spewed plumes of dust across the North Atlantic Ocean and Europe. The highest plume was almost 7 mi (11 km) high and pumped out thousands of tons of ash, grounding planes for a week.

Island of fire and ice

Iceland is an island of extremes. Largely covered in glaciers, it was formed from active volcanoes on the Mid-Atlantic Ridge. About one third of all Earth's lava flows in the last 2,000 years have occurred there.

Mightiest
MOUNTAIN

The Himalayas are not just the biggest mountain range on land, they are also one of the youngest at just 50 million years old. Mount Everest, the highest peak of the Himalayas and in the world, is known as *Chomolungma* in Tibet, and *Sagarmatha* in Nepal.

THE SOUTHEAST RIDGE IS THE MOST CLIMBED ROUTE. IT IS REACHED FROM NEPAL.

MOUNT EVEREST SUMMIT
29,035 ft (8,850 m)

DEATH ZONE
Surviving at altitudes above 26,000 ft is tough, due to low oxygen and freezing temperatures. Climbers who die are often left on the mountain. Eventually, sometimes years later, their frozen bodies are removed for proper burial.

CAMP 4
26,000 ft (8,000 m)

CAMP 1
20,000 ft (6,000 m)

Climbers use a ladder to traverse the crevasse at Khumbu Icefall.

TIMELINE

1841
The location of peak "b" (as Everest was then known) is recorded by Sir George Everest, Surveyor General of India.

1856
Height of peak "b" is calculated as 29,002 ft (8,840 m).

1865
Peak "b" is renamed Mount Everest.

1924
First attempt at climbing Everest fails, though one climber reaches 28,126 ft (8,570 m).

1953
Edmund Hillary (from New Zealand) and Tenzing Norgay (from Nepal) are the first people to reach Everest's summit on May 29.

2007
Retired Japanese teacher Katsusuke Yanagisawa scales Everest at age 71.

KHUMBU ICEFALL
The Khumbu Icefall must be crossed with the aid of ladders and ropes—it is one of the most dangerous parts of the route.

BASE CAMP
On the Khumbu Glacier at 17,700 ft (5,400 m), climbers get used to the altitude before ascending.

EVEREST
29,035 ft
(8,850 m)

K2
28,251 ft
(8,611 m)

KANGCHENJUNGA
28,169 ft
(8,586 m)

LHOTSE
27,940 ft
(8,516 m)

MAKALU
27,838 ft
(8,485 m)

AFTER YEARS OF DISAGREEMENTS ABOUT **EVEREST'S HEIGHT**, CHINA AND NEPAL AGREE IT IS **29,029 FT (8,848 M) HIGH**, INCLUDING 13 FT (4 M) OF SNOW, BUT THE NATIONAL GEOGRAPHIC SOCIETY CLAIMS IT IS **29,035 FT (8,850 M)** TALL.

NUPTSE (peak)
25,790 ft (7,860 m)

LHOTSE (peak)
27,940 ft (8,516 m)

CAMP 3
24,500 ft
(7,500 m)

GENEVA SPUR
Climbers use ropes to scramble over this raised black rock.

CAMP 2
21,300 ft
(6,500 m)

WHAT RUBBISH!

Everest can now claim fame as the world's highest garbage heap. Tourists and climbers are responsible for leaving plastic bottles, food packaging, tents, and even oxygen tanks on the mountain.

Climbers use iceaxes and crampons—metal spikes attached to boots—to scale vertical sheets of ice.

Ultimate
VOLCANO

Earth's crust breaks open and molten rock, ash, and toxic gases spew out of the vent. The awesome force of a volcanic eruption like this hints at the incredible temperatures and pressures that exist far beneath the surface. But what exactly happens to create the ultimate volcano?

▶ In 1980, Mount St. Helens erupted. The top 4,600 ft (1,400 m) of the volcano was destroyed.

VOLCANIC ERUPTIONS ARE MEASURED ON THE VOLCANIC EXPLOSIVITY INDEX (VEI), WHICH RANGES FROM "GENTLE" TO "MEGA-COLOSSAL."

Lava

Rock that has literally melted to a semiliquid state is known as lava. The speed of its flow depends on temperature, and the minerals it contains. One of the fastest lava flows ever measured was from the Nyiragongo volcano in the Democratic Republic of the Congo. It poured out at over 35 mph (60 km/h).

◀ Burning lava flows like a river, and boils the water as it enters the ocean.

Ash

Vast plumes of ash often erupt from a volcano, and can remain airborne for days—and travel great distances—before settling. When Mount Vesuvius erupted in AD 79, a huge column of pumice ash was ejected from the crater at a rate of 1.7 million tons per second. The column reached a height of 2 mi (3.3 km) before collapsing and covering the ground with a suffocating layer of ash.

Eruption

Volcanoes erupt when heat and pressure become too great for the crust to bear, and the huge amounts of energy below the surface are released. In the last of many eruptions in AD 186, a New Zealand volcano ejected an incredible 25 cubic mi (110 cubic km) of rock in one of the most violent eruptions ever recorded. Its crater is now Lake Taupo.

◀ Clouds of ash are carried upward by the force of exploding gas.

Crater

A crater marks the opening of the vent. Lava builds up around it, creating the familiar cone shape. If the cone walls collapse, the crater will get bigger. The volcanoes of Hawaii are among the most active on Earth. Steam and volcanic gases pour out of their craters.

BENEATH THE SURFACE

Molten rock inside the Earth (magma) collects in chambers just below the surface. Heat and pressure force the magma upward, through weak areas in the crust, sometimes until it reaches the surface.

Vent

Conduit (main vent to the magma chamber)

Side vent

Upper magma chamber

Deep magma chamber

Mantle

HOT spots

I n some places, evidence of Earth's extraordinary inner heat comes to the surface. Soaring temperatures bake the rock underfoot, and boil water that lurks within it, causing jets of superheated steam to spurt into the air. Even mud can start to bubble!

Yellowstone

One third of the world's hydrothermal features are in Yellowstone Park in the U.S., which also has more geysers than anywhere else on Earth— 150 of them in just one square mile (2.6 sq km). The whole area sits astride a supervolcano, and while normal volcanoes make mountains, supervolcanoes explode them to smithereens. The most recent eruption was 640,000 years ago, and 1,000 times more powerful than the eruption of Mount St. Helens in 1980. The land continues to reach temperatures of 400°F (around 200°C), and new geysers, mud pools, and fumaroles are constantly created.

Old Faithful

The world's most famous geyser, Old Faithful of Yellowstone Park, U.S., shoots hot water and steam up to 180 ft (about 55 m) into the air. It erupts, on average, every 85–95 minutes because it takes this long for the chamber beneath to refill with water.

The greatest geyser

The tallest geyser ever witnessed existed for only four years, after a volcanic eruption in New Zealand in 1900. Waimangu's jets of black water, rocks, and steam were 1,500 ft (460 m) high—taller than the Empire State Building. Four tourists died in 1903 after being swept away by a sudden, and violent, eruption.

▶ Old Faithful is probably the world's most studied, and best-known, geyser.

▶ Macaques enjoy a hot soak so much they sometimes doze off in the pool.

Monkey baths

Warm water pools created by hot springs in Nagano, Japan, have been adopted by macaque monkeys. They bathe in these natural hot tubs during the freezing winter months.

Cotton Castle

At Pamukkale in Turkey, cascading pools create one of the world's most breathtaking natural wonders. The hot springs, which are rich in minerals, pour down the hillside, filling the pools with warm, blue water. The name Pamukkale means "Cotton Castle."

▶ Pamukkale's hot water pools are created by minerals in the hot water, which turn to stone.

THE GROUND IN SOME VOLCANIC REGIONS IS SO HOT IT CAN TURN MUD INTO BOILING POOLS, AS GASES RISE TO THE SURFACE AND BREAK THROUGH.

CRUNCH Time

Rock is tough but **brittle**, so it's no wonder that the active Earth, **with** all of its subterranean stirrings, puts the **rocky** landscape under more pressure than it can **bear.** When crunch time comes, giant sections of **rock buckle** and slip, creating monumental **movements** that cause Earth's surface to quake and **shatter.**

WHAT'S AT FAULT?

A fault is an enormous crack in Earth's crust, either side of which giant slabs of rock, called tectonic plates, move in different directions. As the slabs slide slowly past each other they may get stuck, causing a buildup of pressure that, when released, results in sudden jolts.

Direction of plate movement

Plate 1

Plate 2

Epicenter

Seismic waves

Focus, or hypocenter

▲ Massive movements along faults release energy around the focus. Seismic waves radiate outward, wreaking destruction in built-up areas.

IN 2010 A QUAKE IN CHILE WAS SO POWERFUL THAT IT LITERALLY MOVED THE CITY OF CONCEPCION 10 FT (3 M) TO THE WEST.

Locals walk along damaged roads as they are evacuated from the earthquake-hit Beichuan County, southwest China, in 2008.

Extreme damage

Major disaster

The 1906 San Francisco earthquake was caused by movement along the San Andreas fault.

Safety measures

A controlled explosion collapses a disused building, simulating an earthquake, and allowing scientists to test a "cage" (red) that would protect people inside.

Predicting quakes

Earthquakes are one of the most catastrophic of all extreme events, yet predicting them remains virtually impossible. Earthquake-proof construction, however, can save lives. Buildings in Japan and California, U.S., are constructed with elastic building materials and shock-absorbing foundations to withstand tremors.

Mega-tsunami

Seafloor shake-up

Tsunamis are caused by sudden, massive movements along fault lines on the seafloor. When faults are close to land, the chance of a mega-tsunami—a high wave of devastating proportions—is greatly increased.

The Indian Ocean mega-tsunami of 2004 devastated the Phi Phi Islands.

GREATEST River

Water from the glaciers and mountains of the Andes pours into the Amazon River at its source.

This waterfall on the Jari River brings water from Guyana's Highlands to the Amazon.

The Urubamba River is an Amazon headwater—a tributary forming part of the Amazon's source.

Rivers have the power to demolish walls of rock and grind them to dust. They have the strength to carry millions of tons of soil and sand, and enough energy to provide electricity for entire cities. There are long rivers, wide rivers, and deep rivers, but by almost any measure the Amazon is the greatest of them all.

A tributary is a river or stream that flows into a larger river. About 200 tributaries flow into the Amazon—more than any other river in the world.

TOP 5 RIVERS

The Nile is generally agreed to be slightly longer than the Amazon, but in terms of volume it's just a trickle by comparison. Every second, the Nile empties 6,600 yd³ (about 5,100 m³) of water into the sea, but the Amazon empties 290,000 yd³ (about 220,000 m³)—43 times as much. That is enough, in one day, to supply a city with fresh water for ten years!

PARANA
23,000 yd³ (about 17,700 m³) of water into the sea per second

YENISEI
25,000 yd³ (about 19,000 m³) of water into the sea per second

YANGTZE
42,000 yd³ (about 32,000 m³) of water into the sea per second

CONGO
55,000 yd³ (about 42,000 m³) of water into the sea per second

AMAZON
290,000 yd³ (about 220,000 m³) of water into the sea per second

During the wet season, the Amazon basin covers 135,000 sq mi (around 350,000 sq km)—an area similar to that of Germany. In the dry season it shrinks by two thirds.

WATER FROM THE AMAZON SUPPORTS THE AMAZON RAIN FOREST, WHICH COVERS 2 MILLION SQ MI (5 MILLION SQ KM). THAT'S TWO THIRDS OF THE AREA OF AUSTRALIA.

River dolphins live in the Amazon's slow-moving, muddy water. They feed on fish and crabs, but little is known about their behavior.

The area of land that is regularly covered by water following seasonal rains is called a floodplain.

THE AMAZON DELIVERS 106 MILLION CU FT (3 MILLION CU M) OF SEDIMENT INTO THE OCEAN EVERY DAY.

As it meets the ocean, extreme surfers take advantage of the unusually long waves (tidal bores) that occur here. It's possible to ride a single wave for 6 mi (10 km)!

The Amazon becomes the widest river on Earth near its mouth—up to 25 mi (40 km) wide in the wet season.

THE AMAZON HOLDS ABOUT 20 PERCENT OF THE WORLD'S TOTAL FRESH WATER.

Extreme
EROSION

On our dynamic planet, nothing remains the same for long. The landscape is continually being molded, eroded, and changed by forces we are scarcely aware of. Human lives are too short for individuals to bear witness to these extraordinary processes, but the remarkable results are all around us.

▲ Hoodoos are tall columns of rock. The rock on the top of a column is harder than the rock beneath it.

A slot canyon is formed by rushing water passing through rock, and eroding a tall, narrow channel.

Sandblasting

In dry places, wind picks up grains of sand and whips them through the air like a sandblaster. The effects can be spectacular. In the Arches National Park of Utah, lofty monoliths, huge arches of rock, balancing rocks, and tablelike mesas stand as monuments in the desert.

▶ The Devil's Marbles, or balancing rocks, of Australia have been shaped by sandblasting.

▼ The eroding power of the Colorado River is responsible for the Grand Canyon, one of the world's greatest natural wonders.

The Colorado River in the U.S. has proved itself the ultimate abrader of rock. Its erosive course began 17 million years ago—the blink of an eye in geological time. Since then it has created a canyon 277 mi (446 km) long, up to 18 mi (29 km) wide, and, in some places, more than one mile (1.6 km) deep, reaching rocks that are 2.5 billion years old.

The Colorado's enormous power of erosion is due to the river's great speed and volume, and the large amount of mud, sand, and gravel it carries. Also, the rocks through which it passes are relatively soft.

▶ The Painted Cliffs in Tasmania are carved by wave erosion, and stained with orange-red minerals.

Breaking waves

In coastal areas, big waves crash against rocks and gradually wear them away in a process known as erosion. The ocean water not only has power and energy to do its work, it also carries grains of sand and mud, which rub away at the rock surfaces. Over time, cliffs are undercut, eventually collapsing into the ocean.

FREEZING

Flow

I n the world's coldest places snow falls but rarely melts. Layer upon layer of it collects, and the fluffy stuff is eventually compressed into dense packs of ice. Huge rivers of ice—glaciers—creep slowly downhill under the force of gravity. As they move, these heavyweight scourers carve a spectacular path through the landscape.

Ice cycles

Glacial ice is constantly melting and freezing, depending on the time of day, the season, and changing temperatures. When more ice freezes than melts, a glacier grows bigger and is said to be advancing. When ice is melting, a glacier shrinks and is described as retreating.

▲ Giant chunks of ice fall from the Perito Moreno glacier into Argentina's largest lake—Lago Argentino.

AGES OF ICE

The global climate is continually changing, and extreme climate changes that lead to ice ages are not unusual. In fact, we are probably experiencing a warm spell during a big ice age even now. During the last ice age so much water was trapped as ice that the world's sea levels fell by 300 ft (about 100 m).

▲ An artist's impression of the landscape and animals of the last Ice Age, about 10,000 years ago. Animals grew thick fur coats as protection against the cold. Many creatures, such as woolly mammoths, survived on plants such as mosses. Others, such as cave lions, were fierce hunters.

> MOST GLACIERS MOVE SLOWLY, BUT THE JAKOBSHAVN GLACIER IN GREENLAND IS REPUTED TO BE ONE OF THE FASTEST FLOWING, MOVING AT A RATE OF AROUND 65 FT (20 M) PER DAY.

◄ The enormous Hubbard glacier reaches into the Gulf of Alaska. It has been slowly advancing for more than 100 years.

Icebergs

When ice sheets and glaciers meet the sea large sections may break off. These enormous frozen chunks float with ten percent of their mass above water because solid water is less dense than liquid water. Drifting icebergs are a hazard to shipping—it was an enormous iceberg that sank the liner *Titanic* in 1912, in which 1,517 people lost their lives.

> THE ICECAP ON THE TOP OF MOUNT KILIMANJARO IN AFRICA IS MELTING SO FAST THAT IT MAY DISAPPEAR WITHIN THE NEXT 25 YEARS.

▼ A colony of penguins hitches a ride onboard an iceberg. They will dive back into the water and hunt for fish when they want to eat again.

A cruise ship is dwarfed by the massive Hubbard glacier

Enter the
ABYSS

A long-term drip of dissolved limestone can build up to create icicle-shaped stalactites

Deep underground, caverns and caves create dark and eerie natural theaters. Dramatic features adorn their walls, and tunnels extend far into Earth's hidden depths. Brave explorers who make the journey underground are often rewarded with awesome sights.

▼ This 30-story-deep sinkhole was caused by heavy rain during a hurricane in Guatemala.

A sinking feeling

Acidic water can create a hole that descends vertically and creates an underwater waterfall. These sinkholes, as they are known, can form suddenly when large areas of weakened rock fall into caverns below. The result can be catastrophic when houses or roads collapse with them.

▲ Drips of water fall to the cave floor and evaporate, and the solid minerals that are left behind build up over thousands of years, creating stalagmites.

Leaky limestone

Most underground caves form in karst landscapes—places where limestone is the dominant rock. As rain and river water seep through limestone it becomes acidic, and dissolves solid rock. The liquid it creates can turn back into limestone, creating stalactites, stalagmites, and other strange features.

Spelunkers

Caves are some of the least explored places on Earth, so there is a special thrill to be had from finding new caves and tunnels to navigate. People who undertake these often dangerous treks are known as spelunkers and pot-holers. The risks they have to be prepared for include cave collapse, hypothermia, falling, flooding, and getting lost.

AT OVER 390 MI (630 KM), MAMMOTH CAVE IN KENTUCKY, U.S., IS THE LONGEST CAVE SYSTEM IN THE WORLD.

▼ Giant crystals of aragonite, a form of calcium carbonate, may develop in some limestone cave systems.

▲ When exploring a cave system, spelunkers may be faced with long stretches of tiny tunnels as well as vast, impressive caverns.

Sizing it up

Cave experts have been mapping a cave network in Sarawak, Borneo, for more than 30 years. By taking measurements using lasers, they have gathered data on over 200 mi (320 km) of the Gunung Mulu network. It contains the world's largest cave—Sarawak Chamber is 2,300 ft (700 m) long and 330 ft (100 m) high.

▼ The gigantic Gunung Mulu caves were only discovered in 1976, beneath a rain forest.

Ancient history

The major mineral in limestone is calcium carbonate, which comes from the shells and skeletons of sea creatures. Over millions of years, the shells and skeletons collected on the seafloor and were, under great pressure, eventually turned into rock.

BURIED
Treasure

Earth's crust contains a treasure trove of minerals that civilization depends upon. Many substances that we take for granted—iron, oil, gold, even talcum powder and the "lead" (graphite) in pencils—are formed in Earth's crust. Extracting them can demand feats of human endurance and technological wizardry.

MARBLE This smooth, strong stone is used in sculpture and buildings.

STEEL A tough metal made by mixing iron with other minerals.

ALUMINUM Strong but lightweight, this metal has many uses.

FLUORITE This pretty mineral is fluorescent (emits light) under ultraviolet light.

DEADLY COLTAN Coltan is a mineral used in the manufacture of cell phones, but extracting it is a life-threatening activity for people in the Democratic Republic of the Congo. Miners use their bare hands to dig, and risk facing collapsing mine shafts, radioactive minerals, and other deadly toxins.

HEMATITE Ground up, this mineral makes a red paint used since prehistory.

MERCURY This liquid metal is used in thermometers to measure temperature.

GRAPHITE Its flexible network of carbon atoms makes graphite very soft.

COAL Burning this fossil fuel releases heat and light energy.

MOST METALS ARE STABLE IN AIR, BUT THE MOST REACTIVE ONES CANNOT EXIST IN PURE FORMS IN NATURE. IF POTASSIUM IS EXPOSED TO AIR, IT REACTS WITH OXYGEN AND EXPLODES.

IN DEEP WATER

When the *Deepwater Horizon* rig exploded in 2010 it killed ten men, sparked the world's largest accidental oil spill, and caused environmental catastrophes. The rig was built to research a reservoir of oil on an area of the seafloor beneath 5,000 ft (about 1,520 m) of water, a challenge that has been described as being more technically difficult than exploring the Moon.

▲ The explosion of the oil rig *Deepwater Horizon* on April 20, 2010 caused an estimated 5 million barrels—210 million gal (800 million l)—of oil to spill into the Gulf of Mexico.

GOLD LEAF Gold is an amazing metal that can be worked more readily than any other. Just 0.03 oz (1 g) can be beaten into 10 sq ft (1 sq m).

NICKEL This silvery metal is used in coins and batteries.

CROWN JEWELS The greatest working collection of jewels includes the Imperial Crown of India, which contains over 6,000 diamonds.

COPPER Can be beaten or rolled into shape, and conducts electricity very well.

DIAMOND Diamonds are made of carbon, which in another form becomes the soft graphite in a pencil lead. It is the hardest known natural mineral, and the most brilliant when cut.

GYPSUM Can be heated to make plaster, used in building, or made into blackboard chalk.

Deep-sea
DIVE

The deep ocean is the world's least explored and most mysterious environment. It is a high-pressure, dark wilderness, so hostile to life that few creatures can survive there. Those that can are bizarre, ranging from colossal squid with eyes bigger than a human head, to glow–in–the–dark fish, and giant worms.

Dumbo octopus
Location: Mid-Atlantic Ridge
Depth: 1,300–13,000 ft
(400–4,000 m)

Journey to the bottom of the sea

In 1960 two explorers, Jacques Piccard and Don Walsh, embarked on one of the most treacherous journeys ever undertaken. Their submersible, the *Trieste*, took them 35,800 ft (10,900 m) into the Mariana Trench, the deepest point of any ocean. To this day they remain the only two people to have made the journey. By contrast, 12 people have traveled to the Moon, which is 238,600 mi (384,000 km) away.

Snow and ooze

Bits of detritus from dead animals and plants are known as marine snow. They drift down to the deep seabed and, over time, build up to create enormous sediments of fine mud and ooze. Some of them are 1,480 ft (450 m) thick.

DeepSee submersible
Carries up to three people to depths of 1,500 ft (about 460 m).

▶ The mineral-rich geysers of water that come from the seabed are called black smokers, and can reach temperatures of 750°F (400°C).

Oasis undersea

The deep sea is a poor habitat for most wildlife, but some places are able to support some of the world's strangest fauna. Fueled by volcanic heat that escapes from cracks in Earth's crust, hydrothermal vents can sustain colonies of limpets, shrimps, starfish, tube worms, and fish.

Giant ostracod
Location: Mid-Atlantic Ridge
Depth: 2,356–6,115 ft (718–1,864 m)

The future

Researching the deep ocean remains one of the great challenges facing science. It is such a perilous environment that humans rarely venture there. ROVs (remotely operated vehicles), such as *Jason*, and AUVs (autonomous underwater vehicles), such as *Sentry*, are now used to enable scientists to explore the seabed from the safety of a ship's deck above.

◀ This image uses colors to show the uneven nature of the Pacific Ocean seabed. The deepest areas appear blue and green. Underwater peaks appear as red and yellow, and mark the East Pacific Rise.

ZONES OF THE DEEP

0 ft

Light Zone Sunlight travels through the water at this level, so plants can photosynthesize (make food), supporting a large range of life-forms.

650 ft

Twilight Zone Dim levels of light can pass through the water, but there is not enough light to support photosynthesis.

3,300 ft

Dark Zone Many animals survive in the inky depths. The seabed is home to sponges, shelled animals, sea cucumbers, and worms.

13,000 ft

Abyssal Zone Fewer animals can survive as the water gets deeper. A great pressure of water bears down on those that do.

20,000 ft

Hadal Zone This is the most mysterious place on Earth, and some strange creatures manage to survive here. Little is known about them.

WILD Winds

Wind is little more than moving air. It is invisible and almost weightless—yet it is impossible to control and is one of the planet's most destructive forces. When winds become high-energy storms, they can develop into hurricanes more than 500 mi (800 km) across—and wreak total havoc.

◄ A spinning tornado collects dirt and grit from the land, turning it into a brown funnel of air.

ON APRIL 3, 1974, THE U.S. ENDURED WHAT IS THOUGHT TO HAVE BEEN ITS WORST EVER TORNADO OUTBREAK, DURING WHICH 150 TORNADOES CAUSED MORE THAN 300 DEATHS AND 6,000 STORM-RELATED INJURIES.

A supercell storm, such as this one in Nebraska, U.S., can produce several tornadoes during a few hours of activity.

Twisting tornadoes

Tornadoes can be deadly, but short-lived. They begin when warm, wet air encounters cool, dry air. In the right circumstances, a vertical column of rotating air forms, which causes a "supercell" that can transform into a vortex of violently rotating wind.

On the move

Air moves because it becomes warm in some places, and cool in others. Warm air molecules have more energy, and move faster, than cold ones. When air moves faster, it expands and rises above cold air, setting up weather systems that sometimes have extreme outcomes.

Storm chasers

Tornado Alley in the Great Plains region of the U.S. is famous for its wild winds, and the storm chasers that pursue them for the thrill, or to gather scientific data. Storm chasers don't just watch the twisters—their goal is to actually go inside them. They follow computer weather models and search for brewing storms. Once in the middle of a tornado, storm chasers rely on their vehicles for protection against high-speed winds, torrential rain, lightning, and giant hailstones.

Hurricanes

The world's greatest storms are called hurricanes, typhoons, or tropical cyclones. They begin at sea and can inflict terrible damage if they move onto land. The worst hurricanes have winds that swirl at more than 155 mph (250 km/h). At this velocity, winds have the strength to rip the roofs off buildings and cause storm surges, when seawater is picked up and hurled inland.

On August 29, 2005, Hurricane Katrina hit land, causing devastating damage in areas such as Kenner, Louisiana, U.S.

IN 1900, A HURRICANE BARRELED THE TEXAN CITY OF GALVESTON, FLATTENING IT AND CAUSING A STORM SURGE AND ONE OF THE U.S.'S WORST NATURAL DISASTERS. AS MANY AS 10,000 PEOPLE DIED IN ONE NIGHT.

Freaky
WEATHER

Weird weather events have long been features of biblical tales and folklore, and have often been attributed to a divine intervention in earthly matters. Scientists have sought to uncover the genuine causes of these oddities, and today they are more likely to be explained by rare, but entirely natural, weather systems.

Cloud art

The study of clouds is called nephology, and for many people it is more of an art than a science. These airborne masses hold water droplets or ice crystals and, owing to climatic conditions, can form some strange shapes. Freaky cloud formations include mushrooms, jellyfish, and donuts!

◄ These puffy clouds, known as mammatus, hang beneath the main body of other clouds and often precede violent storms.

Sun halo

Also called a sundog, this strange atmospheric phenomenon is caused by ice crystals inside high, thin clouds. The crystals reflect light, causing it to shine in a ring, and creating a rainbow that looks as if it is wrapped around the Sun.

Raining fish and frogs

For centuries there have been reports of strange things falling from the sky during storms. These bizarre events are caused by tornadoes, or their watery equivalents—waterspouts. Animals, especially fish or frogs, are swept up into the air, carried some distance, and then dropped during a rainstorm.

▶ A waterspout forms and touches down alongside the Mekong River in Cambodia.

A CHUNK OF ICE MEASURING 7 IN (NEARLY 18 CM) ACROSS FELL FROM THE SKY DURING A STORM IN AURORA, NEBRASKA, U.S., IN 2003.

◀ Lightning striking through a column of volcanic ash produces a dazzling display.

Blue Moon

The Moon may appear blue when forest fires or volcanic ash send tiny particles into the atmosphere where they mix with droplets of water. The mixture is carried by winds and refracts moonlight, causing a blue haze to form.

Fiendish fireballs

About 100 lightning strikes occur around the world every second, slashing through the sky with awesome electrical energy. Balls of lightning, however, are rare events. Fireballs can be the size of a beach ball and they have been seen to pass through windows and walls, hiss, and even explode.

BLUE AND RED FLASHES OF LIGHT ARE KNOWN AS BLUE JETS AND RED SPRITES AND ARE SOMETIMES SEEN ABOVE STORMS. THEY ARE PROBABLY CAUSED BY LIGHTNING IN THE UPPER REGIONS OF THE EARTH'S ATMOSPHERE.

▼ In 2010 parts of Queensland, Australia, were hit by flood waters that covered an area larger than France and Germany put together.

GIVE WAY

STATE EMERGENCY SERVICE

MARINER

Freak floods

Flooding is one of the most common natural disasters on Earth, but flash floods take everyone by surprise. Often caused by a break in flood defenses or riverbanks, following unusually heavy rains or ice-melts, flash floods swamp large areas. In low-lying areas, the effects can be particularly catastrophic.

Ultra FREEZE

Soft, fluffy snow can transform a landscape into a stunning, white wilderness. Yet in its most extreme forms, snow can also bring disaster and destruction. From raging blizzards to colossal avalanches that crash to the ground with the impact of solid rock, the power of snow should never be underestimated.

MOUNT BAKER IN WASHINGTON STATE IN THE U.S. HAD A TOTAL SNOWFALL OF 95 FT (29 M) IN THE WINTER OF 1998-1999.

What is snow?

In cold places—mostly near Earth's poles or at high altitude—rising water vapor can freeze as tiny ice particles in the air. Ice crystals stick together to form snowflakes. The simplest snowflakes are six-sided prisms, but these can branch to create more complex structures. The shape and size of a snowflake depends on the temperature, pressure, and amount of water that is held in the air.

Is every snowflake unique?

Probably yes, although how would anyone ever know? If several trillion ice crystals fell every year, the chance of two identical crystals forming in the lifetime of the Universe is virtually zero.

AVALANCHE SURVIVAL

Mountain rescuers recommend some simple steps to increase the likelihood of survival when out in avalanche-prone areas.

* Check avalanche hotlines and assess the avalanche risk before going into an area.
* If you are skiing or snowboarding, carry an avalanche rescue beacon, which transmits a message to rescue teams.
* You can't outrun an avalanche, but you may be able to run to the side of one.

* If you are knocked off your feet, grab hold of a tree or a rock, or stick your ski pole into the snow.
* Being caught by an avalanche is like being caught in river rapids—the snow will start to pull you under. Try to "swim" through it, and keep trying to make your way to the top of the snow pile.

* When you stop tumbling, clear an area in front of your face so you can breathe.
* Push your arm upward for the best chance of being spotted by someone.
* If you see someone being caught by an avalanche, mark the last point you saw them, so that you—or a rescue team—have a better chance of finding them.

A SEASON OF BLIZZARDS IN WESTERN U.S. IN 1949 LASTED FOR SEVEN WEEKS. DURING THAT TIME MORE THAN 100 PEOPLE, AND ONE MILLION CATTLE, DIED.

Whiteout

A blizzard is a snowstorm driven by winds of 30 mph (48 km/h) or more, where visibility is reduced to 650 ft (200 m) or less. In a severe blizzard or "whiteout," visibility is near to zero.

Hundreds of tons of snow coursing down a hillside can fell trees, crush cars, and demolish houses.

DANGER AVALANCHE

Alpine avalanche

Heavy snow in Chamonix, France, in 1999 caused an avalanche of more than 10.6 million cubic ft (300,000 cubic m) of snow. The flow traveled at 60 mph (97 km/h) until it hit a small hamlet below, destroying buildings and burying people under 100,000 tons of snow. Twelve people died.

The Arctic is a frozen ocean surrounded by continents. During the height of summer in the Arctic Circle, daylight continues for 24 hours. In winter, there is at least one day when the Sun does not rise.

◄▲ Animals that can survive within the Arctic Circle include Arctic foxes and polar bears. The foxes often follow the bears, to feed on the leftover bits of their kills.

▲ Divers explore under Arctic ice, discovering wildlife that survives at the Earth's extreme ends.

The Ends of

THE EARTH

► Animals that can survive in the Antarctic include penguins, seals, whales, and albatross. Shrimplike krill live in the Southern Ocean and are among the most numerous animals on the planet.

The South Pole is on a massive continent—Antarctica—which is covered by the world's largest icecap. With an average area of 5.3 million sq mi (13.7 million sq km), the icecap is one-and-a-half times bigger than the U.S., and holds about 70 percent of the world's fresh water.

Scientists explore ice caves in Antarctica to uncover the region's mysterious past.

A time-delay photograph captures the midnight sun and its reflection in the Arctic Ocean, as it appears to move across the sky.

IN 1958, A SUBMARINE SAILED BENEATH THE FROZEN ARCTIC OCEAN, PROVING THE ICE SHEET RESTS ON WATER, NOT ON LAND.

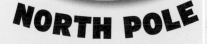

Temperatures in northern Greenland can fall to −94°F (−70°C).

NORTH POLE

SOUTH POLE

IN PARTS OF THE ANTARCTIC THE SUN REMAINS BELOW THE HORIZON FOR 105 DAYS DURING THE WINTER, LEAVING THE LAND IN NEAR-TOTAL DARKNESS.

The coldest temperature ever recorded was at Vostok in the Antarctic. It was −128.6°F (−89.2°C).

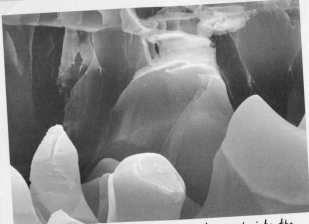

In winter, the Antarctic ice sheet spreads into the ocean, forming layers called ice shelves. Huge ice blocks break off the shelves to form massive icebergs.

Super DRY

Deserts are the world's driest places, where years may pass with no rain at all. They can also suffer extremes of temperature, with hot days and freezing nights. Even the icy Antarctic is classed as a desert. These super-dry places are desolate and often barren—without access to water, few living things can survive.

EARTH'S HOTTEST PLACES

1 Al'Aziziya, Libya
135.9°F (57.7°C)

2 Greenland Ranch, Death Valley, U.S.
134°F (56.7°C)

3 Ghudamis, Libya and Kebili, Tunisia
131°F (55°C)

Las Vegas is a city of excess, but scientists claim it could run dry in the next 50 years.

The desert city

Despite the harsh and inhospitable environment of deserts, one of the world's most successful cities was built in one. Las Vegas, in the American Mohave Desert, is home to 1.8 million people and accommodates 30 million tourists a year. Water is supplied by nearby Lake Mead, but the city is growing too fast for the supply.

In Los Angeles, 140 gal (530 l) a day is required per person—in Las Vegas that figure swells to an unsustainable 307 gal (1,165 l).

A fast-moving wall of Saharan sand and dust, called a haboob, advances on a market in Sudan.

Scorched Sahara

The giant Sahara Desert covers an area equivalent to the U.S., and it is growing all the time. Huge dunes form, reaching heights of 970 ft (300 m), and winds can whip up sandstorms and dust devils. Dust is lighter than sand, and can travel enormous distances.

ARICA IN THE CHILEAN ATACAMA DESERT EXPERIENCED LESS THAN 0.03 IN (0.75 MM) OF RAIN DURING ONE 59-YEAR PERIOD.

Burning up

Wildfires are often started by human activity or lightning strikes, and when they take hold in areas that have endured long, dry periods they can spread by leaps and bounds. Australia has about 15,000 wildfires a year. In 1997, strong winds followed a severe drought in Indonesia, and the result was a massive inferno that raged across 2,900 sq mi (7,500 sq km).

◀ Known as bushfires in Australia, these infernos can rampage through 12 mi (20 km) of vegetation in just one hour.

EARTH'S DRIEST PLACES

RAINFALLS, ON AVERAGE

1. ARICA, CHILE
   ONE DAY EVERY SIX YEARS

2. ASYŪT, EGYPT
   ONE DAY EVERY FIVE YEARS

3. DAKHLA OASIS, EGYPT
   ONE DAY EVERY FOUR YEARS

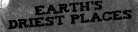

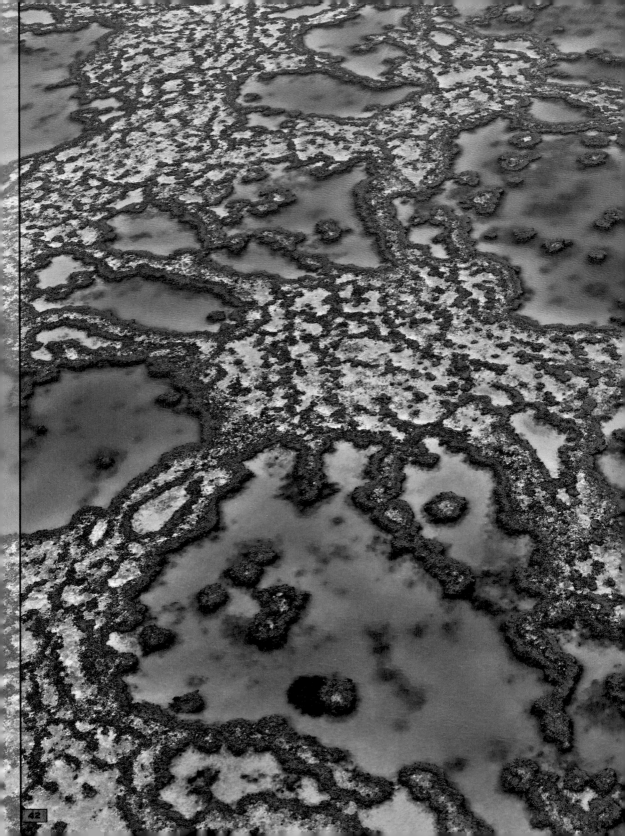

Vast
OCEANS

Journey through Earth's biggest and most mysterious habitat, from the fiery origins of tropical islands to the colossal currents that dictate our climate.

World Ocean 44
Ocean Potion 46
Giant Jigsaw 48
Mega Cold 50
The Ocean Motion Game 52
Super Surges 54
Making the Weather 56
How to Cook an Island 58
From Micro to Mega 60
Mysterious Depths 62
Mega Marine Record Breakers 64
Rhapsody in Blue 66
Seeing in the Sea 68
Treasures and Trash 70
Disaster at Sea 72
Pacific Profile 74
Where Sea meets Land 76

◀ The Great Barrier Reef, on Australia's northeast coast, is possibly the largest structure ever built by animals, covering an area of the Coral Sea that extends for more than 6,500 ft (2,000 m). It took around 18 million years to grow to this enormous size.

WORLD Ocean

Together, the oceans create our planet's biggest environment. With a combined volume of 328,000 cu mi (1,367,200 cu km) of seawater, the world ocean covers about 71 percent of Earth's surface and holds about 97 percent of all global water. It is the largest habitat in the known universe.

THE LANDSCAPES BENEATH THE OCEANS ARE AS DRAMATIC AND BEAUTIFUL AS THOSE ABOVE—FULL OF SECRETS YET TO BE DISCOVERED.

Mega ocean

We separate our planet's water into five oceans and about 20 seas, although they are actually one continuous body of water. The average ocean depth is 12,500 ft (3,800 m). That's the height of 2,500 men standing on each other's shoulders.

BY VOLUME, THE WORLD OCEAN MAKES UP MORE THAN 95 PERCENT OF POTENTIAL HABITAT FOR LIVING THINGS.

The big mystery

Humans have been exploring the oceans for thousands of years, but underwater exploration is a recent activity—more is known about the Moon than about Earth's deep seas. We know oceans represent a huge habitat for wildlife, they affect climate and weather—and that changes in sea level will certainly occur in the future, with enormous consequences for humanity.

The Bahamas are enveloped in sapphire seas, as seen from the Space Shuttle Columbia. From space, the true beauty of Earth's oceans is revealed.

▶ This deep-blue area is part of the Great Bahama Canyon, which is more than twice the depth of the Grand Canyon in Arizona, U.S.

THE ATLANTIC OCEAN IS NAMED AFTER A TITAN OF GREEK MYTHOLOGY—ATLAS, WHO CARRIED THE HEAVENS UPON HIS SHOULDERS. ATLANTIC MEANS "SEA OF ATLAS."

Water origins

Primeval water probably belched out of Earth's rocky layers as vapor in volcanic eruptions about four billion years ago. This vapor created the atmosphere, which cooled and turned to rain. It took millions of years for the oceans to fill. Some water may have arrived in frozen comets that crashed into Earth. Five hundred million years ago, life on Earth was still confined to the oceans.

▲ It is thought that hundreds of millions of years ago, comets and meteorites brought water and minerals to the planet.

THE OCEANS ARE ONE HUGE SHOPPING CHANNEL— MORE THAN 90 PERCENT OF ALL INTERNATIONAL TRADE IS CARRIED ON THE HIGH SEAS.

THE ARCTIC AND SOUTHERN OCEANS ARE THE OLDEST PARTS OF THE WORLD OCEAN.

Who owns the oceans?

Most nations with coastlines have signed up to the Law of the Sea Treaty. This gives them rights and responsibilities for oceans up to 12 nautical mi (13.8 mi, 22.2 km) from the coast. The aim of the treaty is to protect the marine environment and marine businesses, and to keep sea routes open.

Huge manta rays that live in the waters of Indonesia's Komodo National Marine Park are protected by law.

OCEAN
Potion

▼ Ocean water is dense and holds many nutrients, so it's the perfect home for huge animals such as the sunfish, which can grow to a length of 10 ft (3 m).

Water is unique. It is a substance unlike any other on Earth, with the power to give and support life, mold the landscape, and generate an atmosphere. In the oceans, water has some extra-special qualities that help explain why life began there.

Life support

The molecules in water are more dense (tightly packed) than in air. Salty water is denser than fresh water and can support the weight of heavy animals. As water cools, it gets heavier and sinks, so the deep oceans have layers of cold, salty water. When water freezes it becomes less dense, which is why ice floats on water.

▼ Stromatolites are mounds built by tiny organisms that are similar to life-forms that existed about 3.5 billion years ago. They have helped scientists understand how life began in the oceans.

Big soup

Water is the universal solvent, which means that many solids and liquids dissolve in it. Ocean water contains a combination of dissolved gases such as carbon dioxide and oxygen, minerals and salts such as sodium chloride (table salt) and carbonates, nutrients, and microscopic animals and plants. If it could be extracted, there is enough gold suspended in the world ocean for each human to be given a mega 9 lb (4 kg) gold bar!

WHAT IS WATER?

- WATER IS MADE OF HYDROGEN AND OXYGEN MOLECULES.

- HYDROGEN WAS CREATED ABOUT 14 BILLION YEARS AGO (SOON AFTER THE BIG BANG), BUT OXYGEN DIDN'T EXIST IN SIGNIFICANT AMOUNTS UNTIL MUCH LATER—ABOUT 2.45 BILLION YEARS AGO.

- A PINHEAD-SIZE DROP OF WATER CONTAINS ONE BILLION BILLION MOLECULES.

- WE THINK OF OCEAN WATER AS JUST BEING LIQUID, BUT WATER ALSO EXISTS AS VAPOR IN THE ATMOSPHERE ABOVE THE LIQUID OCEANS, AND AS A SOLID AT EARTH'S COLD POLES.

Oxygen atom

Hydrogen atoms

▲ A water molecule—H_2O—contains one oxygen atom and two hydrogen atoms.

Holding on to heat

Water holds heat in a way that air doesn't—so ocean temperatures stay remarkably stable. The upper layers of an ocean are heated by the Sun, but because heat rises this warm water stays near the surface. Below 3,300 ft (about 1,000 m) temperatures drop to a chilly 46–50 °F (8–10 °C).

PACIFIC OCEAN

California

▶ This satellite image taken during a 2004 heatwave in the U.S. state of California shows that the land surface temperature soared (indicated in red), while the oceans (blue-green) stayed much cooler.

THE DEAD SEA IS ONE OF THE SALTIEST BODIES OF WATER IN THE WORLD. IT'S ABOUT ONE-THIRD SALT, BUT IT'S ACTUALLY A LAKE, NOT PART OF THE OCEANS.

GIANT
Jigsaw

Earth's crust consists of giant plates, which are continually moved and altered by subterranean forces. As they expand, shrink, and morph, these plates govern the state of the oceans, which are endlessly created and destroyed.

Phenomenal fissures

The biggest physical feature of an ocean is a mighty fracture in the crust, where two oceanic plates meet and are separating. They are the largest geological features on Earth. Called mid-ocean ridges, these colossal cracks include mountain ranges, formed by molten rock spewing out from Earth's inner layers. As the lava cools, it hardens and grows new crust—making the ocean bigger.

The place where two plates meet, but are separating, is called a **divergent plate boundary**.

One of the fastest-growing mid-ocean ridges, the East Pacific Rise (here in red), grows up to 8 in (20 cm) per year.

Pillow lavas

When lava pours out of cracks under the ocean, it quickly cools to form solid rock. Inside, the lava is still molten and, under pressure, it bursts out to create cushion-shaped rocks called pillow lava. These peculiar forms are common around ocean ridges.

The waters around Kilauea Volcano in Hawaii are a perfect place to see volcanism in action.

Magma from below wells up at a **divergent plate boundary**, adding new rock to the plate margins as they grow.

About 250 million years ago, Earth's continents formed an enormous supercontinent called Pangaea. There was one immense ocean, called Panthalassa. Tectonic forces broke up Pangaea and after 80 million years—at the time of the dinosaurs—the southern continents were combined into one landmass called Gondwanaland, and the mega ocean was divided.

1. Mirovia Ocean 750 mya

3. Oceans today

2. Panthalassa Ocean 250 mya

4. Oceans around Amasia 200 my in the future

The big crunch

When an ocean plate meets a continental plate, the thinner ocean plate sinks. This causes it to be swallowed up, creating a zone of destruction called an ocean trench. A trench can be up to 7 mi (11 km) deep.

For 50 million years, two ocean plates have been on a collision course, creating the Andes mountains.

At a **convergent plate boundary** one plate is forced beneath another. The huge energy involved can cause earthquakes and volcanoes.

As an oceanic plate is forced against a continental plate at a **convergent plate boundary** it gets subducted (pushed down) and usually melts back into the mantle beneath.

Mega COLD

It is so cold at the top of the world that the sea has frozen over. When the ice melts, large pieces of pack ice break away and move through the open ocean. They crash into each other and pile up to make mountainous ice ridges.

An epic sea change

Scientists are predicting that the next supercontinent—Amasia—will see the closing of the Arctic Ocean. Around 100 million years from now, the monumental movements of Earth's continental blocks could see the Polar north covered in land as the Americas and Asia crash into each other.

DURING THE LAST ICE AGE, SO MUCH OF EARTH'S WATER WAS FROZEN THAT THE SEA LEVELS FELL BY 330 FT (100 M).

THE BIGGEST ICEBERG EVER MEASURED WAS 550 FT (NEARLY 170 M) TALL—ONLY A LITTLE SHORTER THAN THE WASHINGTON MONUMENT IN WASHINGTON D.C., U.S.

Ice grows and floes

In winter, Arctic sea ice grows thicker and wider, and can reach about 5.8 million sq mi (15 million sq km). Sheets of floating ice are called floes. Large masses of floating ice are called icebergs—meaning "mountain of ice." Most of an iceberg's great bulk is hidden beneath the sea surface. Very large icebergs are sometimes known as "ice islands."

▼ Polar bears of Svalbard, in the frozen Arctic, rely on ice floes to survive—this is where they can find the seals on which they feed.

5 ICEBERG MEGAFACTS

1 Icebergs float in the oceans, but they began life as ice on land, or as part of ice sheets.

2 Iceberg ice is collected and sold to be served in drinks. The air trapped inside the ice may have been there for more than 3,000 years.

3 Melting icebergs leak nutrients into the water—scientists have found that the water around them often teems with marine life.

4 The International Ice Patrol was set up to warn ships of the danger of floating ice after *Titanic* hit an iceberg and sank in 1912.

5 A huge iceberg was named B-15. Its total area was about the same as Jamaica!

Arctic thaw

The Arctic sea ice is experiencing a dramatic thaw. It is losing about 190,000 sq mi (about 500,000 sq km) per decade. Earth's climate has always undergone huge changes over geological time, but the current changes in global temperature are a major cause for concern. If the Arctic continues to thaw at this rate, global sea levels will rise—causing widespread flooding.

▼ The yellow line indicates the minimum amount of Arctic ice expected in August each year. The white region shows the actual amount of ice on August 26, 2012.

Fjord coastlines

During the Ice Age, huge glaciers were common much further south of where they exist today. When the world warmed and the ice retreated, huge valleys that had been carved by the glaciers became flooded with seawater. These features are called fjords and they are particularly common in northerly areas such as Scandinavia and Canada.

▼ Massive glaciers carved their way through the landscape that is now Baffin Island in the Canadian Arctic, creating beautiful fjords.

NORTH VS. SOUTH

ARCTIC	ANTARCTIC
Polar ocean—the North Pole is covered in sea ice.	Polar land—there is no sea ice at the South Pole itself.
Frozen ocean that stays frozen in parts.	Frozen land with areas of sea ice surrounding it in winter.
Sea ice is up to 15 ft (5 m) thick.	Sea ice in the Southern Ocean is typically 3–6 ft (1–2 m) thick.
The Arctic Ocean is frozen, so it rarely rains or snows.	Rain and snow are common in and around the surrounding Southern Ocean.

THE OCEAN Motion GAME

Go on the journey of a lifetime as you join massive movements of water far below the ocean surface. It's the Global Conveyor—the largest long-distance movement of water on the planet, with more than 100 times the flow of the mighty Amazon River.

CURRENT AFFAIRS

The force of winds whipping the water's surface, combined with flows of cold (blue) and warm (red) water, create gyres (giant circular surface currents) in every major ocean basin. Though they only affect ten percent of ocean water, gyres have a huge impact on our weather.

North Atlantic Gyre

TAKE ANOTHER TURN

CURRENT AFFAIRS

The top 10 ft (3 m) of the ocean holds as much thermal energy as Earth's whole atmosphere. Currents move thermal energy in warm tropical water toward the cooler north and south. Where warm and cool currents collide, in places such as the Cape of Good Hope, they create storms.

GO FORWARD THREE SPACES

CURRENT AFFAIRS

Scilly Isles

CURRENT AFFAIRS

CHANCE

ATLANTIC OCEAN

QUIZ

Cape of Good Hope

CURRENT AFFAIRS

CHANCE

PACIFIC OCEAN

The Global Conveyor stops parts of the ocean getting too salty, hot, or cold, and distributes nutrients and gases. If rain in the North Atlantic increases due to global warming, it will warm Arctic sea ice and stop the sinking of cold water, slowing the Conveyor. The mild climate of the Scilly Isles is among the conditions under threat.

GO BACK FOUR SPACES

One massive movement of ocean water is vertical. Water cools near the poles, and sinks. As it warms up again, it moves upward, bringing food for plankton, which then undergo giant growth spurts. Animals swim up through the water column to feast on plankton near the surface.

PICK ANOTHER CARD

GIANT CONVEYOR

The Global Conveyor is a massive circulation of water around the planet.

It moves like an enormous conveyor belt, heating and cooling as it goes. Cold water is heavy, so it sinks at the North Atlantic, then heads south to the Antarctic. From there, it moves up into the Indian Ocean and Pacific, where it heats and rises as it becomes less dense. Much of this water is moving far beneath the surface.

PACIFIC OCEAN

INDIAN OCEAN

CURRENT AFFAIRS

WARM SURFACE FLOW

COOL SUBSURFACE FLOW

SOUTHERN OCEAN

QUIZ

FOR AN EXTRA THROW, ANSWER THIS QUESTION:

If you followed one drop of water as it travels on the Global Conveyor, how many years would it take you to return to the starting point?

ANSWER: 1,000 YEARS

CHANCE

YOU'VE BEEN SWEPT UP IN THE AGULHAS CURRENT— ONE OF THE LARGEST MOVING BODIES OF WATER IN THE WORLD. IT FLOWS AT TOP SPEEDS OF 6.6 FT/SEC (2 M/SEC).

Super
Surges

The surface of an **ocean** is in permanent turmoil. Waves can be big and brutal, but **tides** have a much more impressive **power** behind their strength. We owe our ocean tides to events in space, and the pulling power of the Sun and the Moon.

▼ Most places have a high tide every 12.5 hours, as well as monthly tidal patterns. The biggest tides, spring tides, are caused when the Sun, Earth, and Moon align. Their combined gravitational pull results in the movement of enormous masses of water.

Moon

Neap tides
In the first and third quarters the gravitational pulls of the Sun and Moon oppose each other, producing neap tides

Sun

Moon

Spring tides
At new and full Moon, the gravitational pulls of the Sun and Moon combine, producing spring tides

Sun

The tide is high

Tides are the result of three mega-celestial movements: Earth orbiting the Sun, Earth spinning on its own axis, and the Moon orbiting Earth. Their combined forces literally pull the oceans away from Earth's center. At high tide, the sea level rises. At low tide, it drops.

SEA OF tranquility

The Sargasso Sea is 2 million sq mi (5.2 million sq km) of serenity. It's part of the Atlantic and often experiences very calm, current-free conditions. As a result, island-sized mats of Sargassum seaweed up to 10 ft (3 m) deep thrive, and support big communities of ocean wildlife.

▲ Loggerhead turtles are ~~visibly~~ endangered, but their young enjoy some ~~protection~~ from sharks and humans in the Sargasso Sea.

When wind moves over water, it stirs it up and creates ocean waves. A light wind causes ripples, but stronger winds up to 40 mph (60 km/h) create high waves and rough seas. The distance between the peaks of two waves is called a wavelength, and large waves can have a wavelength of 1,000 ft (300 m) or more.

▶ The seas south of Cape Horn in Chile, where the Atlantic meets the Pacific, are famously wild.

▼ A surfer braves giant waves at Pe'ahi (also known as "Jaws" because the waves are so dangerous) in Maui.

California Beach
Original
Boarding

The big surf

Waves break as they reach the shore and their energy explodes into frothy white surf. Big wave surfing is popular at Jaws Beach in Maui, Hawaii. Massive swells here lead to mega waves of 60 ft (18 m) or more in height, and fast-moving crests. Tube riders ride through the middle of a giant wave, while the crest breaks rapidly from the left or right above their heads.

MONSTER WAVES

• Every now and then, a freak event occurs and a random mega wave rises out of an ocean swell. Known as monster, rogue, or killer waves, these extraordinary events have the power to snap large boats in two.

• The highest storm wave ever to be encountered occurred in 1933 when the USS Ramapo was traveling from the Philippines to San Diego, U.S. One wave was calculated as 112 ft (34 m) high, traveling at 75 ft/sec (23 m/sec).

• Between 2000 and 2013, there were 263 freak wave accidents in Taiwan, which resulted in the deaths of about 100 people.

Making the WEATHER

Air, water, and the Sun's radiant heat give us our wild and wonderful weather. Most of the planet's water and solar energy is stored in the oceans, so it's no wonder they play a crucial role in creating the world's weather systems.

Cumulonimbus (storm) clouds can have a total height of more than 6 mi (10 km), and a single colossal cloud may contain up to **250,000 tons** (227,000 tonnes) of water.

The water cycle

Every drop of water on the planet is part of a giant circular movement called the water cycle. It is one of our planet's biggest and most important systems. The Sun provides the energy that fuels this movement of water.

Around **85%** of evaporated ocean water falls back into the oceans as rain—the rest reaches land before condensing.

In Guadeloupe, in the West Indies, an incredible 1.5 in (38 mm) of rain fell in just **one minute** in November 1970.

PRECIPITATION
Droplets get bigger and water falls as rain, hail, or snow.

CONDENSATION
Water vapor cools to a liquid state and creates clouds.

RUNOFF
Water is carried downhill by rivers, and into the ocean.

EVAPORATION
The Sun warms water on land and ocean, turning it into vapor.

TRANSPIRATION
Water vapor is produced by plants.

INFILTRATION
Water seeps into the ground and flows to the ocean.

UNDER PRESSURE

The Sun warms a vast expanse of ocean, and the air above it warms too—and rises. These simple steps may be the beginnings of a tropical storm, or even a hurricane...

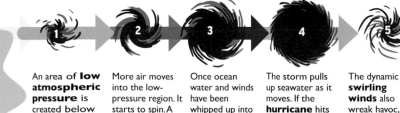

1 An area of **low atmospheric pressure** is created below the mass of warm air, and clouds **form** above it.

2 More air moves into the low-pressure region. It starts to spin. A **circular wind system** forms and becomes a tropical storm.

3 Once ocean water and winds have been whipped up into a **tropical storm** frenzy, they are ready to do damage.

4 The storm pulls up seawater as it moves. If the **hurricane** hits the coast, this seawater surges, flooding and eroding the coast.

5 The dynamic **swirling winds** also wreak havoc, but eventually lose their energy.

INSIDE A HURRICANE

From above, these giant weather systems look like masses of swirling clouds, but a great deal is happening beneath the surface.

Falling cold air

Eye
The eye has the lowest pressure and is relatively calm, with no rain and even clear skies

Cloud patterns
The swirling clouds form a distinctive ribbed pattern when seen from space

Rising warm, moist air

Rainfall
Many inches of rain can fall in a few hours around the eye of a storm

Rotation
Wind patterns in the area, plus the Coriolis Force due to Earth's rotation, usually start the whole hurricane spinning slowly

Winds
Powerful air movements are set up within the storm

HURRICANE CATEGORIES

Category 1
VERY DANGEROUS

Category 2
EXTREMELY DANGEROUS

Category 3
DEVASTATING

Category 4
CATASTROPHIC

Category 5
VERY CATASTROPHIC

Super energy savers

If we didn't have such big oceans, our summers would be much hotter and our winters would be much colder. Oceans store energy well, so they help to thermoregulate the planet. That's why the average temperatures at the North Pole (which is surrounded by ocean) are higher than those at the South Pole (which is surrounded by land). Even though thick layers of sea ice form at the North Pole, the sea underneath remains liquid.

The coldest ocean water is a frosty **28°F (-2°C)** in the polar oceans, and the warmest is a sizzling 97°F (36°C) in the Persian Gulf.

In winter the ice over the Arctic Ocean reaches **15 ft (5 m)** thick. In summer it shrinks, but it never disappears completely.

How to Cook
an ISLAND

The lush tranquility of tropical islands conceals their turbulent pasts—they form in hellish heat and violent underwater explosions. Volcanoes are named after Vulcan, the Roman god of fire, and when they erupt at sea they produce burning torrents of lava, which release sulfurous steam as they sizzle and cool. These impressive events may give birth to brand new islands.

Preparation:

Ocean volcanoes are created in three main zones.

Grow Zones
Black basaltic lava spews from ocean ridges and the ocean floor spreads and widens. A ridge may be the site of many volcanic islands.

Crush Zones
When two ocean plates are on a collision course, one gets sucked under the other and destroyed. Volcanoes often form along these massive crush zones.

Hot Zones
Hotspots form when heat from Earth's innards is concentrated in certain areas. The heat melts the rock, and volcanoes form. Earth's plates are always moving, so a volcano moves on from the hotspot, and a new one forms. Eventually, a whole chain of volcanoes forms but only the youngest, nearest the hotspot, is active.

Method:

1 FIRST FIRES
Earth's crust fractures and the explosive power of a volcano emerges from the seafloor. Lava spews out from the volcano's superheated foundations of magma (molten rock). The surrounding seawater is heated to colossal temperatures.

▲ *An underwater volcano erupts near Tonga. Plumes of steam, smoke, and ash make their way to the sea's surface.*

2 AN ISLAND IS BORN

A volcano continues to erupt and grow as lava hardens into rock and adds to its height. Eventually, the volcano's crater is above sea level. Over time the lava and ash combine to make a fertile soil and animals and plants become established.

▼ *Ash rises into the air from an undersea volcano, part of the tiny islet of Hunga Ha'apai near Tonga.*

UNDERWATER ERUPTIONS ACCOUNT FOR MORE THAN THREE-QUARTERS OF EARTH'S TOTAL MAGMA PRODUCTION.

TIPS

The slopes of a volcano or guyot (see below) provide the right conditions for coral habitats to become established, and are home to animals such as this stone scorpionfish.

3 TIME TAKES ITS TOLL

Over time, the volcano becomes inactive. The sea erodes the island until it disappears. Beneath the waves, a flat-topped seamount is left. It is now called a guyot, after Princeton's first geology professor.

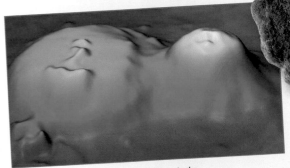

▲ *A 3D model of Ferdinandea volcano in the Mediterranean Sea shows its twin peaks. It has grown and eroded several times.*

From Micro to Mega

Coral islands and barrier reefs are big enough to be seen from space, and yet they are created from the labors of billions of tiny animals that are often smaller than a fingernail. These giant structures are incredibly complex, based on an intricate network of relationships between a wildly diverse and numerous range of living things.

Critical coral

Coral reefs only take up about one percent of the world ocean, but they are a marine habitat of almost incomparable importance. A single reef contains countless places for animals to live, hide, and hunt. As a result, reefs contain an incredible one quarter of all known types of sea creature, and are a home for billions of organisms.

Coral reefs are among the oldest ecosystems in the world. Reef-building corals have existed for more than 210 million years.

▼ The Maldives are home to the seventh largest coral system in the world and the two largest atolls.

Atoll story

There are three main types of coral reef: fringing, barrier, and atoll (coral island)—although some places have a mixture of all three. Atolls are the result of volcanic activity—once a volcano has disappeared, a beautiful circular structure (the atoll) may be all that's visible in a clear turquoise sea. A blue, shallow lagoon forms in the middle of an atoll.

▶ The development of a coral atoll can take at least 100,000 years.

1. Coral polyps establish their reef-building colonies in the shallow water fringes of a volcanic island.

2. As waves erode its surface and the sea floor sinks, the island slowly disappears beneath the waves. The corals keep building their ring upward so the reef's upper part stays at the surface.

3. The fringing reef continues to grow, creating an atoll and a beautiful blue lagoon.

Big bang theory

It was the natural historian Charles Darwin (1809–1882) who first suggested that coral atolls could have formed around long-gone volcanoes. He was proved right in 1942 when a deep hole was drilled into the Bikini Atoll and it reached volcanic rocks at the bottom. The Bikini Atoll achieved notoriety when it became a nuclear bomb test site in 1946, and when a two-piece swimsuit was named after it!

◀ An image from Charles Darwin's work *The Structure and Distribution of Coral Reefs* shows a coral island.

Mighty Maldives

The Maldives lie in the warm Indian Ocean. A submerged volcanic mountain range is surrounded by 26 atolls, and between them they contain about 1,200 coral islands, reefs, and sandbanks. The capital, Malé, is built on an island that is part of an atoll, but the average height above sea level of the entire island chain is only 5 ft (1.5 m). If sea levels rise significantly, the Maldives would disappear beneath the waves.

Big builders

Coral polyps are fussy animals and only thrive in certain conditions. They require warm, clean, salty water, solid rock to grow on, and plenty of sunlight. They secrete a mineral-rich substance in a cup-shape around their soft bodies. Over time these cups collect to create a geological structure, such as Australia's Great Barrier Reef.

▲ A yellow coral polyp extends its feeding tentacles into the water. They capture tiny drifting animals.

▲ The Maldives' Baa Atoll contains 75 islands — 57 of which are uninhabited.

MYSTERIOUS DEPTHS

DEEP-SEA ZONE →

Some of Earth's most impressive, massive, and extensive features lie beneath the ocean's surface. Sadly, we will never be able to see them in the inky depths, because even submersible lights can only illuminate tiny areas.

▼ Dumbo octopuses live near the seafloor at great depths. They swallow prey whole.

▲ Deep-sea yeti crabs have hairy claws. They live around hot vents.

THE WORLD'S BIGGEST HABITAT

The deep ocean begins at about 650 ft (200 m) below the surface of the sea, and extends to its dark, gloomy bottom. It is the largest habitat on Earth, taking up about 80 percent of its available space. Despite this, it was long believed the deep ocean was devoid of life. Now we know it's home to a huge variety of animals, which have adapted to life in a lightless, high-pressure environment.

▼ Pteropods are swimming mollusks with winglike flaps. They live around sea cliffs and canyons.

THE DEEP-SEA LANDSCAPE →

The destructive power of rivers continues deep under the sea. They carve huge canyons through the seafloor, and deposit great quantities of sediment. At around 13,000 ft (4,000 m) deep, the ocean floor spreads out in one flat layer—the abyssal plain. It accounts for half the ocean floor and is the single biggest environment on Earth. Silt, mud, sand, and dead animal remains have collected here over hundreds of millions of years, reaching depths of up to 3,300 ft (1,000 m).

▲ Jiaolong is a manned submersible. Its robot arms collect sediment at depths of more than 4.4 mi (7 km).

Written in stone

Two hundred million years of recorded geological and biological history of Earth are found in the ocean's floor. By studying ocean sediments and rocks, scientists can learn about ancient climate, how it changed, and how better to predict our own climate.

Super-heated water

Around undersea volcanoes and ocean ridges, where Earth's inner heat escapes, ocean water gushes out of structures called hydrothermal vents at up to 750°F (400°C)—the temperature of molten lead. The pressure is so great that it does not turn to steam. The super-heated water holds colorful minerals dissolved from the crust, creating underwater fountains known as black or white smokers. The minerals then build into chimneys; one of the tallest found so far is Godzilla at 148 ft (45 m) high—the height of a 16-story building.

▶ Thousands of giant red tubeworms and squat lobsters cluster around a black smoker.

Trenches in turmoil

When an ocean plate meets a continental plate, the ocean plate is destroyed, and a deep trench is formed at this dynamic meeting point. These ocean trenches are the deepest places on the planet's surface.

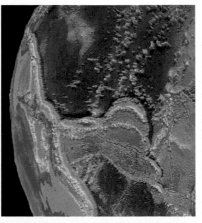
▲ A computer model shows the topography (physical features) around the Mariana Trench (purple), the deepest point on Earth.

MEGA MARINE
Record Breakers

The oceans are the biggest expanses of water in the known Universe, the largest habitats on Earth, and the most mysterious places on our planet. It is no wonder they are home to many mega record breakers!

Everest
29,029 ft
(8,848 m)

Sea level

Mauna Kea
32,696 ft
(9,966 m)

Sea floor

Tallest mountain: Mauna Kea

A mountain is usually measured from sea level to summit, making Mount Everest's peak the highest point on Earth. But if you measure from base to summit, volcanic island **Mauna Kea is much taller than Mount Everest!**

Deepest diver: Sperm Whale

Marine biologists have tracked sperm whales as they have descended through the oceans to inky-black depths of **3,900 ft (1,200 m).**

Strongest tidal current: Saltstraumen 25 mph (40 km/h)

When tidal water is forced into a narrow channel, it can create ferocious maelstroms (whirlpools) strong enough to rip apart boats and pull objects to the seabed. The world's strongest maelstrom, in Saltstraumen in Norway, is made up of several pools that shift as the tide waxes and wanes. It travels at 25 mph (40 km/h) and has a diameter of 33 ft (10 m).

These huge cetaceans also have the biggest brains in the world— 17 lb (7.7 kg). *That's 100 times the weight of a dog's brain!*

Saltiest marine water: Red Sea

Water here is about **ELEVEN TIMES** saltier than most ocean water.

Biggest animal:
Blue whale

The blue whale is the biggest animal that has ever lived on Earth. It weighs up to 200 tons (180 tonnes)—twice as heavy as the biggest estimate for any dinosaur, and its blood vessels are big enough for a child to swim through.

The blue whale's heart is the size of a small car.

At 98 ft (30 m) the blue whale is more than twice the length of a *T Rex*.

Biggest plant: Giant kelp

One of the biggest and fastest growing plants in the world makes up huge undersea forests. A single piece of giant kelp can grow to 100 ft (30 m) in length. That's equivalent to three double-decker buses end to end.

Highest wave:
Alaska, 1958

1,720 ft (520 m)– that's taller than a 100-story building.

In 1958, an earthquake resulted in a massive rockfall in Alaska that triggered the world's largest wave. The impact of millions of tons of rock crashing into a narrow bay caused a massive "splash," which turned into a wave of gigantic proportions. The wall of water swept up the bay, ripping millions of trees out by their roots as it reached its peak.

One World Trade Center in New York City, U.S.

RHAPSODY IN BLUE

Underwater, the seas seem almost silent to us, but we miss out on an incredible world of sound. Many marine animals are able to both make and hear sounds. We are only just starting to understand the impact of sound on the ocean environment.

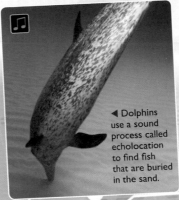

◄ Dolphins use a sound process called echolocation to find fish that are buried in the sand.

Sounds of the sea

Sound travels through salt water at about one mile per second (1.5 km/s)—that's about five times faster than in air. It can also travel great distances, which is of great use to underwater mariners, and to the big beasts of the oceans. We find it hard to hear sounds underwater because our ears are designed to hear sound waves in air.

Surround sound

Undersea mining makes an enormous amount of noise and disturbs wildlife. One solution is to surround oil-drilling machinery with a curtain of bubbles. The bubbles stop the sound waves from traveling—and the whales can enjoy some peace and quiet.

◄ Researchers at the University of Texas, U.S., investigate the properties of bubble curtains in reducing noise pollution.

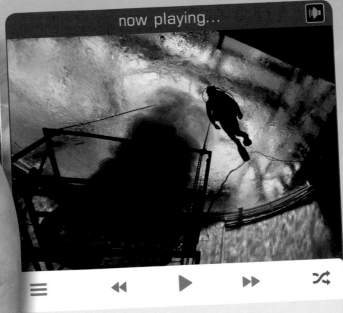

now playing...

Ocean water absorbs radio waves, which is why cell phones can't work under the sea, even if they are waterproof!

SOFAR so good

There's a broad band of water 0.6–1.9 mi (1–3 km) deep where temperature, salinity, and pressure are optimal for channeling sound. Known as the SOFAR (SOund Fixing And Ranging) Channel, the strange, low-frequency sounds here are the calls of baleen whales that swim in this band when they want to communicate.

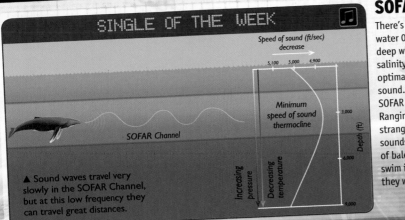

Speed of sound (ft/sec) decrease

5,100   5,000   4,900

Minimum speed of sound thermocline

Depth (ft)

3,000

6,000

9,000

Increasing pressure

Decreasing temperature

SOFAR Channel

▲ Sound waves travel very slowly in the SOFAR Channel, but at this low frequency they can travel great distances.

Seeing with sound

Sonar is a sound system used to detect and measure objects underwater, and calculate depth. The process involves sending sound waves out toward the unknown object. They "bounce" back from the object and these "reflections" can be measured to calculate size, shape, and distance. Animals such as bats, whales, and dolphins use a similar system, called echolocation.

▶ In this sonic image of the continental shelf off California, U.S., white areas are shallowest and blue areas are deepest.

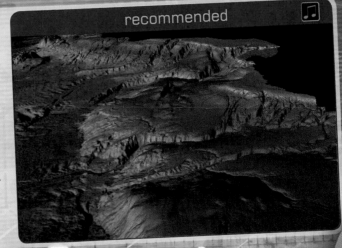

recommended

Explosive exploration

Sound is being used to search for deposits of oil and gas. Seismic air guns fire blasts of compressed air through the ocean and into the seabed. The echoes are used to find reserves of hydrocarbon fuels. The impact these sounds may have on marine wildlife is not fully known.

◀ Seismic air guns are lowered into the sea, where they will make dynamite-like explosions.

coming soon

SEEING in the Sea

The breathtaking **sights** of an ocean include myriad shades of blue, **glow-in-the-dark octopuses,** and scarlet shrimps. But things look the way they do for a reason—**there is science behind** the splendor and **serenity of** a vast body of **water.**

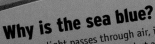

Light penetration in open ocean

Depth (ft)

100
200
300
400
500
600

▲ Some light can penetrate to depths of about 3,300 ft (1,000 m) but most of it has disappeared at just 650 ft (200 m).

Why is the sea blue?

When sunlight passes through air, it contains all the colors of the rainbow, but as it moves through water, it changes. The water begins to filter out different wavelengths (colors). Red and yellow are the first to go, and eventually only blue light is left. By depths of about 0.6 mi (one kilometer), most light waves have disappeared, leaving an eerie darkness.

Glow in the dark

A little light goes a long way in the pitch-black deep sea. Some animals are able to glow, thanks to bioluminescent bacteria. Being luminescent has some advantage—it tempts inquisitive prey to come close, and it may help advertise an animal's presence to potential mates.

▶ Flower hat jellyfish are able to emit glowing colors using wavelengths in the blue to ultraviolet part of the light spectrum.

At the surface

The color of ocean water has been described in many ways: authors have referred to it as "snotgreen," "brown spume," or "sapphire blue." Large bodies of water appear blue because they absorb red light, and reflect blue light. Near the shore there are more particles of rock, mud, and silt suspended in the water, making it cloudy or brown. But its degree of blueness is also down to the color of the sky above it—the sea is like a giant mirror, reflecting blue or gray skies.

Turquoise is caused by weaker absorption of red light

Plankton blooms can cause water to appear bright green

Rain and wind produce darker, foamy seas

Black and blue

Aquamarine seas can surround giant oceanic sink holes. These areas of black and blue indicate columns of icy water that descend deeper than the surrounding sea—the water is still, cold, and dark. Exploring these strange ocean features can be hazardous—visibility may be low and they may contain toxic layers of water.

▲ The Black Hole of Andros in the Bahamas is a huge sinkhole that contains no oxygen, just like the oceans 3.5 million years ago.

Red not dead

Lots of deep-sea animals are red—this color doesn't spell danger underwater; it works like an invisibility cloak. At the surface, a red fish's body reflects red light waves, and appears red. At depth, few red light waves can penetrate so there is no red to reflect. The fish's body absorbs all the other light waves of color and appears black, blending with its surroundings.

▲ A deep-sea opossum shrimp appears a stunning scarlet to us, but it is invisible to deep-sea predators.

Treasures and

TRASH

Oceans provide us with great riches, from minerals to a seemingly endless supply of food. Yet they are an ecosystem like any other—and humanity has taken precious little care of them. The health of the oceans is inextricably linked with the future of our race.

Tipping the balance

For millennia, humans have used the oceans to dispose of their waste. In recent times, industrial waste has added to the ocean's problems. The marine environment is regularly polluted with pesticides, herbicides, nitrogen-rich fertilizers, detergents, oil, sewage, and chemical waste from pharmaceuticals and other industries.

▼ Phosphates are used in fertilizers. Waste products from North African phosphate factories are pumped directly into the sea.

Throwing it back

Commercial fishing techniques include trawl nets that can be up to 200 ft (60 m) across. They scoop everything up from the seafloor, and unwanted—but now dead—animals are thrown back. It is thought that, globally, a staggering 30 million tons (27 million tonnes) of captured marine life is discarded every year.

▼ Trawlers targeting prawns for human consumption also take catsharks and crabs from the sea.

Dirty dumping

People have been dumping their waste into the seas for centuries. Today, it is estimated that 80 percent of all the waste we dump at sea is made of plastic. The main problem with plastic is that it does not biodegrade. It simply breaks up into smaller and smaller pieces, and gets ingested by billions of animals, from whales to plankton.

▲ It is easy for a green sea turtle to mistake a plastic bag for food, and swallow it.

THE LAST TIME OCEAN CARBON DIOXIDE LEVELS ROSE DRAMATICALLY, MILLIONS OF SPECIES WERE WIPED OUT.

Ocean riches

It's not just fish we take from the sea. The oceans contain many other treasures such as sea sponges (a type of animal) and pearls, which are produced by oysters. Pearls occur naturally, but cultured (farmed) pearls now dominate the industry.

▲ Fijian villages rely on pearl farms for income and jobs, but the pearl-producing oysters can be badly affected by marine pollution.

The oil age

Modern humans mostly rely on fuels that come from oil, coal, or gas. Oil and gas are extracted from massive reservoirs beneath the oceans. It is an expensive and risky business, but a highly profitable one.

▲ Oil rigs drill wells deep into the seabed and extract oil. It is used to make fuel and plastics.

BOTTLE BOAT

In 2010, environmentalist David de Rothschild sailed with a small crew across the Pacific in a catamaran made from 12,500 empty water bottles. He aimed to show how plastics can be recycled usefully, not dumped into landfill and the oceans. The journey took 128 days and covered 8,000 mi (12,900 km).

▲ Plastiki arrived in Sydney Harbor after a journey made solely using renewable energy.

Huge harvest

Traditional sustainable fishing has long since been overtaken by a vast commercial fishing industry. The total annual commercial harvest from the seas now exceeds 94 million tons (85 million tonnes) and fish are probably the biggest source of dietary protein in the world.

▼ Indian mackerel live close to shore, making them easy to catch in waters around Southeast Asia.

DISASTER AT SEA

Most of Earth's cataclysmic events happen at sea. Many occur under water, and we may never even notice them, but some have a profound effect on the lives of people who experience their deadly effects. Experts warn that future global ocean activity could put more lives in jeopardy.

HURRICANE HELL

In 1780, one of the deadliest hurricanes on record raced across the Atlantic Ocean and more than 20,000 people were killed when it reached the Caribbean Sea.

Even stone buildings gave way to the fury of the winds and collapsed, crushing thousands. More than 40 ships in the path of the cyclone were sunk with their crews. The velocity of the winds stripped bark off any tree left standing.

As seen in this 2007 photo of Hurricane Dean, these mega storms intensify in the Atlantic, then move west toward the Gulf of Mexico and the Caribbean.

Hurricane season is in September, when the Gulf of Mexico and the Caribbean can be dangerous places to be. More Category 5 hurricanes occur here than anywhere else.

Mega tsunami

Unexpected movements in Earth's tectonic system can have catastrophic repercussions. A convergence of the oceanic Nazca plate and the South American plate to the west of Chile caused a megathrust earthquake in the ocean to the west of the country. It triggered a massive tsunami, which traveled widely, from Alaska to Australia, and claimed the lives of more than 500 people.

This devastation was caused by a massive earthquake in Chile on February 27, 2010, and the tsunami that followed about 30 minutes after the quake.

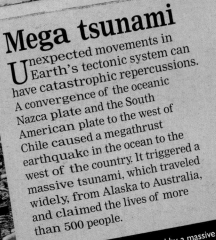

Volcanic wipeout

Just two survivors are left alive on the once idyllic island of Martinique. They alone can recount the story of the explosion of Mont Pelee—the volcano that is now believed to have brought death to 30,000 people in just two minutes. Read their exclusive story inside…

In 1902 Mont Pelee exploded and destroyed the town of St. Pierre, engulfing it with toxic gas, ash, and red-hot rock.

The Baltic Sea's ecosystem has been damaged by pollution to such an extent that large parts of it are considered "dead."

Danger lurks in the real "Dead" Sea

Tourists have long enjoyed the delights of the Baltic Sea, but the future of this resort is looking not just gloomy—it's looking toxic. The Baltic is largely cut off from the main oceans, making it Earth's largest area of brackish water. Dumping of farm waste and sewage has altered the sea's ecology—and massive blooms of tiny plants, called phytoplankton, are turning the water into a foul green soup. Nothing else can live in the oxygen-free zone, and experts are now warning swimmers to stay away.

PACIFIC
Profile

The Pacific Ocean is bigger than all of Earth's land combined. As well as being record-breaking in its volume and depth, this stupendous seascape contains an awesome variety of habitats, beautiful vistas, mega tectonic activity, and so much more.

Sea level

Mariana Trench
35,797 ft
(10,911 m)
deep

Mount Everest
29,029 ft
(8,848 m) tall

OCEAN DEEP

The average worldwide ocean depth is about 12,460 ft (3,800 m). Its lowest point is Challenger Deep in the Mariana Trench of the Pacific Ocean, at 35,797 ft (10,911 m). If Mount Everest were put in the Mariana Trench, it would still be submerged beneath 1.2 mi (2 km) of seawater!

The Ring of Fire includes
452
volcanoes.

SHRINKING SEA

While the Atlantic and Indian oceans are growing, the Pacific is shrinking. It has a high number of subduction zones, where the ocean crust is being swallowed up and melted down. It loses about 0.2 sq mi (0.5 sq km) a year.

ALEUTIAN TRENCH

Most of the Pacific lies over one tectonic plate—the Pacific Plate. Its boundaries are marked by the Pacific Ring of Fire, home to 75 percent of all volcanoes and 90 percent of earthquakes. The most northerly part is created by the subduction of the Pacific Plate under the North American Plate, giving rise to the Aleutian Trench. In 1912, Alaska's Mount Katmai was the site of one of the largest volcanic eruptions of the 20th century.

Sea of Okhotsk

Bering Sea

Kuril Trench

Emperor Seamounts

Philippine Sea

Mariana Trench

The area of the Pacific is more than four times the area of the **Moon.**

Mariana Trench

• Challenger Deep

About **60%** of all fish that are caught come from the Pacific.

Coral Sea

Tasman Sea

Exxon Valdez

▶ Workers try to clean oil-covered rocks on the shore of an Alaskan island, after the _Exxon Valdez_ disaster.

Mount Katmai

Aleutian Trench

Northeast Pacific Basin

Hawaiian Ridge

A POWERFUL PLACE

The Pacific harbors vast reservoirs of oil and gas—the South China Basin alone may contain at least 11 billion barrels of oil and 611.4 cu mi (2,548 cu km) of gas. Extracting and moving carbon fuels can be hazardous. One of the Pacific's most devastating disasters occurred in 1989 when oil tanker _Exxon Valdez_ struck a reef in Alaska Sound. The resultant spill polluted 1,300 mi (2,100 km) of coastline. Efforts to remove oil from the shore and save wildlife took months, and were of limited success.

There is an unnaturally high level of caffeine in the Pacific. It gets there from human sewage that has flowed into the ocean.

The Pacific has a coastline of about **84,500 mi (136,000 km).**

▼ The dense kelp forests of the Californian coasts are the perfect habitat for sea otters.

Central Pacific Basin

East Pacific Rise

Easter Island

SUPER STATUES

Easter Island is one of the Polynesian Islands. It is famous for its culture, epitomized by huge stonework sculptures. People settled here long ago, but their overuse of the island's limited resources led to their own demise.

Half of the Pacific seabed is covered in red clay that has come from the land.

OCEAN HOME

The Pacific contains some of the world's most important marine wildlife sanctuaries, including Monterey Bay, the Gulf of California, the Galapagos Islands, the Tubbataha Reefs, and Komodo Island.

Where sea meets 👉 LAND

Coastlines are among the most active places on Earth, constantly carved by the power of the waves and molded by weather. A coastline marks where land meets sea, and coastal communities are as varied as their geology.

In mangrove swamps the line between land and sea is blurred by marine forests. The Sunderbans of India is the world's largest mangrove swamp. The swamp has formed in the Bay of Bengal, where three river mouths meet. It covers about 1,500 sq mi (3,900 sq km) and is a unique habitat for more than 40 species of mammal—including the Bengal tiger.

MASSIVE MANGROVES

A chital deer finds food, such as fruit from mangrove trees, in the Sunderbans. The trees thrive even though the water is salty.

Delta belters

Soil and other sediments from the River Danube pour into the Black Sea, creating a vast wetland habitat in a delta that is growing at the rate of 79 ft (24 m) per year. About 330 species of bird inhabit this wetland ecosystem, including 70 percent of the world's white pelican population.

THALASSOPHOBIA IS A FEAR OF THE SEAS AND OCEANS.

The Aval Cliffs in Étretat, France, are chalk. Erosion has created sheer faces and natural arches.

The Danube Delta is a UNESCO World Heritage Site, recognized for its outstanding beauty and ecology.

Beaches are created from sandy deposits, and they often give rise to spectacular sights. The longest spit (a long sandbar) is the Arabat Spit of the Ukraine, with a length of 70 mi (113 km). The Great Dune of Pyla, in France, is the tallest sand dune in Europe. It reaches a height of 351 ft (107 m) and draws one million visitors each year.

Dungeness Spit, in the U.S. State of Washington, is one of the world's longest spits, at 5.5 mi (8.9 km) in length.

Big BEACHES

SHALLOW SEAS

Shallow coastal seas may not always look spectacular, but their tranquility often hides a rich environment beneath the surface. Rocky, sandy, and muddy seabeds create a range of habitats for animals, plants, and algae. As the seas flow in and out with the tide, rock pools are submerged and exposed, creating unique, but challenging, habitats.

Wind and waves constantly lash at coastal rocks, and bizarre landforms can result. Sea stacks, arches, and collapsing cliffs bear testament to the incredible power of the oceans to change the landscape. Storm waves of 33 ft (10 m) can erode chalk cliffs by 3 ft (one meter) in just one night.

HIGH ENERGY

Plants and algae photosynthesize and thrive in the shallows, creating a refuge for animals such as this spiny seahorse.

Earth's WONDERS

Embark on a whirlwind global tour and be inspired by the majesty of Earth's extraordinary natural features.

Mighty Monolith	80
Rock and Awe	82
Symphony of Spectacles	84
Cradle of Life	86
Wild Wetland	88
White Out	90
Dragon's Jewels	92
Pinnacles and Pillars	94
Smoke that Thunders	96
Carnival of Coral	98
Valley of the Moon	100
Ice Mountains	102
Wildlife Hideaway	104
Frozen Kingdom	106
Big Island's Fire	108
Emerald Scene	110
Wonder No More	112

◄ On average, 38,500 cu ft (2,000 cu m) of water flows over the Victoria Falls every second, creating a mighty roar that can be heard up to 25 mi (40 km) away.

Mighty
Monolith

Uluru rises majestically above a flat desert horizon in central Australia. Also known as Ayers Rock, this giant red monolith creates such an awesome spectacle—especially at dawn and dusk—that it is central to the religious faith of the indigenous people.

Island mountain

Uluru is the tip of a massive rock slab that is buried to a depth of 4 mi (6 km). Its complex history began 900 million years ago when sediments began collecting in a depression in Earth's crust. Now it is one of the last witnesses to some mammoth geological processes, including the weathering and erosion that have removed the surrounding rocks. These forces will, one day, also erase the mighty Uluru from the landscape.

▶ Uluru is composed of arkose, a type of sandstone rich in quartz and pink minerals called feldspars. The reddish color of the rock is heightened by iron oxides.

Sacred site

The local indigenous Aborigines (the Anangu) are the Traditional Owners of Uluru. They hold the area as sacred and caves at the rock's base are decorated with carvings and paintings that form part of a faith system for one of the oldest human societies in the world.

▶ Indigenous art uses symbols such as concentric circles, and animals such as kangaroos that share the land. It is used in ceremonies and storytelling.

FORMATION OF ULURU

Long ago, mountains were eroded and produced deep layers of sediment. Around 500 million years ago these sediments were drowned by a sea, covered with more sediments, and compressed to become arkose. By 300 million years ago, the arkose had been tilted upwards. Since then, the softer surrounding rocks have been eroded.

▢ Arkose (a type of sandstone)
▢ Proterozoic sedimentary rocks
▢ Igneous and metamorphic rocks
▢ Paleozoic rocks

Rectangle indicates position of Uluru over time

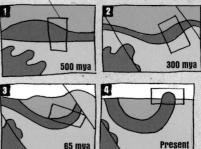

1 — 500 mya
2 — 300 mya
3 — 65 mya
4 — Present

SUN SPECTACULAR

Uluru is known for its astonishing beauty at sunrise and sunset, when the rock takes on a luminous orange glow. As the Sun's rays pass through the atmosphere, they are filtered by dust, ash, and water vapor, especially when the Sun is low in the sky. Blue light rays are blocked, leaving the red end of the light spectrum to illuminate the rock. Uluru's natural red tones intensify the phenomenon.

12 noon

Sunset

Less light is filtered

More light is filtered by atmosphere

The rock contains pink feldspars and red iron oxides

Earth

Many Heads

About 20 mi (32 km) west of Uluru lie 36 steep-sided rock domes. Their Aboriginal name—Kata Tjuta—describes the peaks as "Many Heads." Formed at the same time as Uluru, they are also revered as sacred sites. The largest rock, Mount Olga, gives Kata Tjuta their alternative name—The Olgas.

▼ The resistant rock of Kata Tjuta contains gravel, pebbles, and boulders all held together by a natural cement.

THE DEEP LINES THAT SCORE ULURU'S SURFACE ARE CAUSED BY WIND AND RAIN, WHICH ARE GRADUALLY WEARING AWAY THE ROCK.

Big rock at Burringurrah

Also known as Mount Augustus, Burringurrah is twice the size of Uluru, and much older. This solitary peak is one of the largest rocks in the world with a height of 2,400 ft (around 720 m). It stretches for 5 mi (8 km) and natural springs at its base have long supported the Wadjari Aboriginal people.

▼ The scrubland and waterholes around Burringurrah create a wildlife paradise where gum trees, wildflowers, reptiles, bustards, and even emus thrive.

ROCK
and Awe

▼ Viewed by satellite, the mighty Colorado River looks like a meandering stream within the snow-covered chasm that surrounds it.

The Grand Canyon is a scar on the face of Earth that is visible from space. This long, wide, and very deep chasm is a slice through our planet's mind-boggling history—and it is still growing.

Rainbow rocks

The Grand Canyon forms part of an incredible vista at any time of day, but as the Sun settles behind the distant horizon its fabulous colors become even more evident. Pale pinks and lilacs give way to brilliant reds and neon oranges while the sky becomes an inky wash. Golden light and deep shadows emphasize the canyon's countless ridges, pinnacles, and valleys, highlighting the colossal scale of this breathtaking panorama.

Howdy hoodoo

It's hard to imagine that bizarre amphitheaters of rock populated by needlelike pinnacles (hoodoos) were once vast plateaus of solid rock that have been sculpted by erosion and the weather. Bryce Canyon (below) was named after a pioneer who built a ranch there in the 1870s and remarked that it was a terrible place to lose a cow!

▼ The tallest pinnacle at Bryce Canyon is called Thor's Hammer and is a popular spot for tourists viewing a spectacular sunset.

▲ The view from Toroweap Outlook takes in the Inner Canyon and its heart—the Colorado River.

THE GRAND CANYON COVERS FOUR ERAS OF GEOLOGICAL TIME, FIVE HABITATS, AND FOUR DESERT TYPES, AS WELL AS UNIQUE FOSSIL AND ARCHEOLOGICAL RECORDS.

◄ Californian condors are one of the largest bird species in North America, with a wingspan of 9 ft (around 3 m). They are also one of the world's rarest birds.

Welcome home

For millions of years, Californian condors have soared over the canyon. They search for carcasses to feed on, making the most of thermal air currents that help them glide effortlessly over long distances. A range of threats, including poisoning and habitat loss, saw their numbers plummet to just 22 individuals in 1982. The condor remains an endangered species but a captive breeding program, and reintroductions to the wild, have resulted in condors once again flying above the canyon.

ELECTRIC DISPLAY

A summer's evening at the canyon can become a spectacle of flashing light and rumbling thunder, as storms brew and electrical charges build in the intense heat. Lightning strikes somewhere in the canyon around 26,000 times a year, and each bolt may split dramatically in the sky, forking toward the ground and striking points up to 5 mi (8 km) apart. It usually hits areas of high elevation, especially trees that line the rim. Dead and scorched skeleton trees around the canyon's highest edges bear testament to nature's grim power.

A slice in time

The Colorado River, which carved the canyon, is almost out of sight as it continues its ancient path through the rocks. As it flows, the river has sculpted a deep chasm through layers of sedimentary rocks, exposing bands of color. The top layers are just 260 million years old, while at the bottom, the river has reached rocks that are one mile (1.6 km) down and almost ten times older.

SYMPHONY
of Spectacles

People have been shaping their habitats for millennia, and nowhere is this more evident than Rio de Janeiro, Brazil. Situated in one of the most spectacular landscapes on Earth, this is a bustling modern city where nature's beauty provides the awe, and sweeping urbanization packs the punch.

Peachy beaches

Tourists throng Rio's world-famous coast, enjoying the sunshine and sea along the magnificent 2.5 mi (4 km) crescent of white sand that is Copacabana Beach. Here, waterfront hotels, shops, and restaurants are as much part of the scenery as the backdrop of forest-covered hills.

RIO DE JANEIRO

▼ Citizens of Rio, or *Cariocas*, flock to Copacabana Beach in the day to play, swim, and laze in the sunshine, but in the evening, partying takes over.

◀ Sugarloaf Mountain is 1,299 ft (396 m) tall and juts into the sky at the tip of the bay's peninsula.

Landmark peak

Rio is generally agreed to be one of the most stunning harbor cities in the world. Built on a series of hills, Brazil's carnival city is still flanked by swathes of virgin forest and enjoys a stunning view over Guanabara Bay and granite islands. Sugarloaf Mountain, however, has long been the area's iconic feature and is still an ideal landmark for sailors approaching Rio after an arduous journey across the Atlantic.

CABLE CARS HAVE FERRIED ABOUT 37 MILLION VISITORS TO SUGARLOAF SINCE 1912. THEY ENJOY THE JOURNEY OF A LIFETIME AND PANORAMIC VIEWS OF RIO AND ITS BAY.

Rocky Corcovado

Corcovado is a huge granite peak named after the Portuguese word for "hunchback." Both Sugarloaf and Corcovado are volcanic formations that were once underground. Over hundreds of millions of years, the softer rock on top wore away, leaving these strange rocks exposed as steep-sided mountains—so steep that soil cannot form so they remain bare rock. Where the sea has flooded into the gaps between the granite islands as sea levels rose, beautiful curving bays are created.

▲ Tourists visiting Christ the Redeemer have the best views over the city and bay. The statue was built in the Art Deco style and completed in 1931.

CRADLE
of Life

One of the most striking natural wonders of the world, the Great Rift Valley extends from Jordan to Mozambique. This enormous system of valleys, lakes, plateaus, mountains, and volcanoes is home to millions of animals and contains Olduvai Gorge, an area of Tanzania regarded as the cradle of human life.

AFRICA

SHIFT AND SHAKE

The Great Rift Valley is the ever-widening gap between two vast tectonic plates that are moving gradually apart. Starting in southwestern Asia, this dramatic steep-sided valley cuts through East Africa, completely dividing every country it passes through. The valley and its landforms extend for 4,000 mi (around 6,500 km) and are also known as the East African Rift System. Already in the north, the sea has flooded in to form the Red Sea—and eventually East Africa will separate from the rest and the Rift Valley will be an ocean.

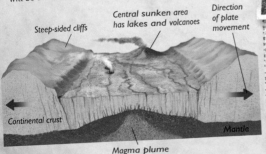

Steep-sided cliffs

Central sunken area has lakes and volcanoes

Direction of plate movement

Continental crust

Mantle

Magma plume

▲ Upwelling heat in Earth's mantle forces plates apart and causes plenty of volcanic activity along the valley floor. As the plates move, brittle rock is put under enormous pressure and breaks along fault lines.

▼ The grasslands of the Ngorongoro Crater are home for many Maasai people, who practice nomadic pastoralism.

Ngorongoro Crater

In the southern region of the Great Rift Valley lies the Ngorongoro Crater, the remains of an extinct, collapsed volcano. At up to 14 mi (22.5 km) across and 2,000 ft (610 m) deep, it is the world's largest complete and unflooded caldera (collapsed volcanic crater). Its steep sides help to create the crater's own weather system, and within its "walls" a unique ecosystem exists. The wildlife here is largely isolated from bigger populations that live beyond the Ngorongoro.

▼ Kilimanjaro's tallest peak reaches 19,340 ft (5,895 m) and is the highest point in Africa.

EGYPT

RED SEA

ERITREA

SUDAN

DJIBOUTI

ETHIOPIA

East African
Rift Zone

SOMALIA

UGANDA

KENYA

Lake
Victoria

Mount
Kilimanjaro

Ngorongoro
Crater

Lake
Tanganyika

DEMOCRATIC
REPUBLIC OF
THE CONGO

TANZANIA

Lake
Malawi

MALAWI

MOZAMBIQUE

ZAMBIA

Peak icing

A volcanic massif (group of mountains), Kilimanjaro is formed mostly from three large extinct volcanoes. The youngest volcanic cone, Kibo, retains an ice cap all year but global warming and deforestation are having a dramatic impact on the massif's iconic icing, which may soon disappear.

The remains of the first tool-using human ancestor, Homo habilis, and early man, Paranthropus bosei, are some of the anthropological treasures discovered at Olduvai Gorge in the Rift System, leading scientists to believe that human evolution began in this region.

▼ Lake Malawi provides a range of habitats for wildlife, from deep clear water to sandy beaches and wooded hillsides.

Great Lakes

The western branch of the Rift System hosts the African Great Lakes, where the rift filled with water. Lake Malawi is known for its great size, the clarity of its water, and the astonishing biodiversity it supports—it contains the largest number of fish species of any lake in the world. Lake Victoria is Africa's largest lake by area and is the source of the White Nile. Long, slender Lake Tanganyika is the second deepest lake in the world.

Wild **Wetland**

The Pantanal is **the** largest-known freshwater wetland in the world, and it is **a** paradise for animals and plants. It extends from Brazil into Paraguay **and** Bolivia, covering at least 50,000 sq mi (129,500 sq km)—an area bigger than 29 of the U.S. states.

Seasonal soakings

An immense low-lying floodplain, the Pantanal contains some areas that are permanently swamped wildernesses. During the seasonal soakings, when rains in the nearby highlands pour into the river systems, the rivers burst their banks and the area underwater increases to around 80 percent.

Super habitat

Seasonal flooding sees a peak in fish breeding in the swampy plains, but during the dry season, from May to September, large areas of land are exposed and dry out. Grazing animals move in, closely followed by their predators—jaguars. Wading birds feast on the fish left exposed in isolated pools and a diverse range of animals feed among giant lily pads and water hyacinths.

▼ Spectacled caimans are the most adaptable of all crocodilians, so they can tolerate the Pantanal's changing conditions.

▼ There are at least 50 species of reptile in the Pantanal. Yellow anacondas give birth to their young in water.

▼ Floodwaters on the Pantanal can reach 13 ft (4 m) in height during and after the long summer rainy season, creating challenging conditions for cowboys and their herds.

Alien invaders

Cattle have been grazing on the Pantanal for around 260 years and many millions are now kept on enormous ranches. Large areas of woody vegetation have been removed using the cut-and-slash method, or by burning, to produce more grazing land.

▲ An incredible array of wildlife lives on the Pantanal, including the world's largest rodents, capybaras, which have a body length of about 3.3 ft (1 m). They are adept swimmers.

Adios Pantanal?

The Pantanal has been described as "one of the last intact ecological paradises." However, cattle ranching, commercial hunting, and pollution are just a few of the growing threats to this habitat. While some recent large-scale plans to turn the Paraguay River into a more navigable route for cargo have been put on hold, other projects planned for the rivers and tributaries that feed the wetlands are still being developed. This is likely to increase the environmental pressures that already face this precious ecosystem.

"PANTANAL" MEANS "SWAMP," BUT ACTUALLY THE REGION IS A PLAIN, AND THE REMAINS OF AN ANCIENT INLAND SEA THAT IS SLOWLY DRYING OUT.

WHITE Out

The astonishing all-white vista created by a large salt flat makes for a formidable sight. These dried-out lakes are some of Earth's flattest surfaces, and the salt crystals that cover them reflect the Sun's rays to create glimmering, shimmering spectacles.

All dried up

Salar de Uyuni is a huge windswept salt flat high on Bolivia's Altiplano (high plain). It is found at an elevation of 11,995 ft (3,656 m) above sea level and covers an area of 4,085 sq mi (10,580 sq km). Beneath several feet of salt lies a salty pool of water that belonged, around 40,000 years ago, to a much larger body of water—the prehistoric Lake Minchin. Over time, heat has evaporated the water, allowing salt to precipitate out as a solid. Salar de Uyuni receives seasonal flooding, and when covered in a thin film of water it creates one of the world's largest natural mirrors.

Pass the salt

The high concentration of salt in these lakes creates an inhospitable environment, although a few species manage to survive. Salar de Uyuni also supports human life in the form of mining communities and tourism. The mined salt is used in building materials. In the future, mining may concentrate on extracting vast reserves of lithium, which lies beneath the salt-encrusted surface. This soft metal is used primarily by ceramics and glass industries, and in the production of batteries.

◄ Giant cacti grow on Inkahuasi Island, a rocky outcrop in Salar de Uyuni. They have a dense covering of spines, which are modified leaves, and flower periodically.

▲ Salt is shoveled into small piles, then transported by truck.

Tiny islands

While the salt plain is almost perfectly flat, there are protrusions that rise above its pristine white surface. These rocky outcrops near the middle of the lake are the remnants of volcanoes that existed on the plain before being flooded by the ancient Lake Minchin. They contain fossils that provide evidence of this region's submerged history, and today they provide an oasis in the sea of vast, blinding whiteness. On these islands hardy animals and plants can survive, including cacti. When the lake is flooded, South American flamingos also visit, to feed and breed.

◄ As the Sun slides toward the horizon, the sheets of white salt take on a stunning blue hue, and rock islands create strange shadows.

SALAR DE UYUNI IS THE WORLD'S LARGEST SALT FLAT, AND THE DIFFERENCE FROM ITS LOWEST PARTS TO ITS HIGHEST PARTS IS NO GREATER THAN 3 FT (80 CM).

TRAIN CEMETERY
Old train tracks connect the lake to the nearby town of Uyuni. Cargoes of salt were taken from the lake to the town by train, and onward to ports. The locomotives are no longer used, but have been left to decay in an area known as the "train cemetery."

DRAGON'S
Jewels

At Halong Bay, on the border of Vietnam and China, geology and mythology combine to create a mysterious seascape of limestone pillars, islands, and islets. It was once believed that these strange rocky outcrops were placed there by dragons to defend the land from invasion.

The water in Halong Bay is mostly less than 30 ft (around 10 m) deep, and covers a drowned karst plain.

Drowned rocks

During Earth's history the sea level has risen and fallen after the planet's climate has undergone large changes. When seawater is trapped in ice the sea level falls; when global warming occurs the ice melts, and the sea level rises. It was this process that caused the sea to invade a karst (limestone) mountain landscape on the Vietnamese coast, in an area now called the Gulf of Tonkin, and create Halong Bay. The strange shape of the islands comes from the way that limestone is dissolved by acidic rainwater. Today, the bay contains more than 2,000 islands, each covered with virgin jungles. They are still largely uninhabited and unspoiled.

▼ As acid rain erodes the islands they can develop into unusual shapes, giving rise to their local names, such as "Elephant" and "Wallowing Buffalo."

Jade and jewels

According to ancient legend, Halong Bay was formed when the region was under invasion, and dragons came to defend the land. As they descended from the sky, the dragons spat out thousands of pearls. Each pearl hit the water and turned into a jade island, and together the islands created an impenetrable barrier to the invading ships.

Caves of awe

Marine erosion has continued to shape and form the landscape, carving out many more caves and grottoes, adding to those created before the coast was flooded. Hang Sung Sot ("Cave of Awe"), for example, is one of the oldest caves in the area and has passages that are more than 33 ft (10 m) high and wide that lead downward to caves filled with stalagmites and boulders.

THE TOWERS OF LIMESTONE HAVE NEAR-VERTICAL SIDES. ROCKFALLS ARE COMMON AND HUGE SLABS OF ROCK OFTEN PEEL OFF AND SLAM INTO THE SEA BELOW.

THE INVADING SEA

Rain falling on limestone creates acid, which dissolves the rock and creates tunnels, caves, and shafts called sinkholes. When the sea invades, this "drowned karst" landscape is the result.

Older caves formed when the sea level was higher

Hills

Chasm

Tower

Recently formed cave

Drowned chasm

PiNNaCLEs
and Pillars

When the world's weathering processes get to work, the landscape can be utterly transformed. Changes in air temperature, and moisture and chemicals in the atmosphere, can carve strange pillars, columns, and pinnacles from solid stone, producing a spectacular range of scenery.

▼ Parts of Cappadocia's bizarre landscape are protected within the boundaries of the Goreme National Park in Turkey.

Fairy chimneys

In Turkey's Cappadocia region, thousands of conical structures appear to rise out of the ground, reaching up to 165 ft (50 m) in height. These are the remains of a vast blanket of volcanic ash that solidified into a soft rock called tuff. Over millions of years, erosion has removed much of the tuff and sculpted these towers, which are known as fairy chimneys. More resistant rock forms mushroomlike caps on some of them.

Twelve Apostles

Coastal rock stacks are witnesses to the immense ability of the sea to carve solid rock. The Twelve Apostles in Australia are limestone stacks that stand along a high-energy coast. They were once part of a large limestone bed that has been slowly demolished by wind, waves, and rain. They continue to disappear at a rate of one inch (2.5 cm) a year.

▲ Australia's Twelve Apostles were originally known as The Sow and her Pigs, before being renamed in the 1950s.

The Needles

When Lot's Wife, a 120 ft (37 m) sea stack in coastal waters by the Isle of Wight, collapsed into the sea during a storm in the 18th century, it was said that the sound could be heard miles away. Lot's Wife was tall and thin, which is why the group of sea stacks it belonged to are known as The Needles, even though the three remaining stacks are quite stumpy. A lighthouse clings to the furthermost Needle, to warn shipping of the collapsed stack below the waves.

▼ The Needles in southern England are formed of chalk, a soft, white limestone.

Moonscape on Earth

The Pinnacles Desert in Australia has a spectral quality, and it is often compared to a scene from a science fiction movie. At sunset the stone structures rise from a bed of golden sand and are set against a sky that is washed in pinks, golds, and lilacs. The Pinnacles were formed recently in geological time and they are the remains of a limestone bed that has been eroded, chemically changed by rainwater, and further altered by plants.

▲ The tallest structures in the Pinnacles Desert are 11.5 ft (3.5 m) tall.

Bald Heads

The large balancing boulders at Matobo Hills in Zimbabwe have been called Ama Tobo, or Bald Heads. They are made of granite, which formed under intense heat and pressure during a volcanic mountain-building phase. Cracks in the rock have helped the elements erode the boulders into these strange shapes. Cecil Rhodes, the founder of Rhodesia—now Zimbabwe and Zambia—is buried here.

▼ Stacks of rocks defy gravity at Matobo Hills.

Smoke that THUNDERS

Falling sheets

The Victoria Falls is neither the tallest nor the widest waterfall, but it can lay claim to producing the largest single sheet of water in the world. In full flood, during February and March, more than 18 million cu ft (500,000 cu m) of water cascades over the precipice every second. Sited at the border of Zambia and Zimbabwe, the falls span nearly 6,000 ft (1,800 m) at the widest point, and have a maximum drop of 355 ft (108 m).

▼ The Victoria Falls cascades over the lip of a large rocky plateau. The mass of water has been slicing slowly through this rock for two million years.

As the mighty Zambezi River plunges over a vertical cliff-edge, a thunderous roar fills the chasm below. A vast, white veil of mist plumes upward, giving the Victoria Falls its local name of *Mosi-oa-Tunya*, which means "The Smoke that Thunders."

Gouging gorges

After the water pummels the rocks at the bottom of the Victoria Falls, it continues its journey through a narrow zigzag series of gorges, passing seven points where the falls were once sited. Water erosion continues to gouge out weaker areas in a vast plateau of basalt rock, moving the falls further and further up the river's course.

▶ After descending the falls, the wide Zambezi is forced through a long zigzag series of extremely narrow chasms, increasing the speed and force of the water's flow.

Devil's Pool

Tourists flock to the Victoria Falls and, when the river levels drop, those looking for an adrenaline rush can enjoy the surreal—and risky—experience of bathing on a cliff edge. The Devil's Pool has a natural rock wall that (in theory) prevents swimmers from being dragged over the top by the raging water's momentum.

▲ Low water levels between September and December allow tourists to enter the Devil's Pool and swim perilously close to the falls' edge.

THE VICTORIA FALLS IS ABOUT TWICE AS WIDE AND DEEP AS THE NIAGARA FALLS. ITS SHIMMERING MIST CAN BE SEEN MORE THAN 12 MI (20 KM) AWAY.

Angel Falls

The best way to appreciate the awesome spectacle of the world's tallest falls is by air. In fact, the Angel Falls in Venezuela was named after U.S. pilot Jimmy Angel, who got a bird's-eye view when he crash-landed nearby in 1937. The Churún River gushes over the Angel Falls at such a rate that water scarcely touches the cliff face as it plummets 3,212 ft (979 m).

▲ In Venezuela the Angel Falls is known as *Kerepakupai Merú*, which means "waterfall of the deepest place."

CARNIVAL of Coral

The enormous size of the Great Barrier Reef needs a long-distance view because its thousands of individual reefs and islands stretch for over 1,240 mi (2,000 km). Getting to grips with its astounding impact on nature, however, means going underwater.

▼ The reef is made up of 3,000 smaller reefs and 1,000 islands.

Slow-grow

A reef is a slow-growing structure of rocky carbonate compounds and the living coral polyps that create them. Australia's Great Barrier Reef is the planet's most extensive coral-reef system and one of the largest structures ever made by living things. The reef has been growing for 18 million years. The living parts, which are growing on top of the older sections, began forming after the last Ice Age, 8,000–20,000 years ago.

▲ Yonge Reef is a popular part of the Great Barrier Reef for divers because of the huge diversity of its corals and other wildlife.

1. Planula searches for a place to settle

▼ Polyps can reproduce in two ways. An egg can grow into a planula, or an adult can make a bud, which grows into a twin of itself.

4. Coral colony begins to grow through "budding"

3. Polyp begins to grow a stony cup

2. Planula attaches to a hard surface

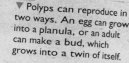

Critical critters

Coral polyps are soft-bodied animals related to sea anemones. They live in extensive colonies and secrete minerals to create protective cups around themselves. It is these cups that make up the bulk of a reef structure. Corals that grow near the surface in sunlit waters have a symbiotic relationship with zooxanthellae algae. The corals provide the algae with carbon dioxide, nutrients, and a safe place to live; the algae give the corals sugar and oxygen from photosynthesis.

THE SINGLE BIGGEST THREAT TO CORAL REEFS IS THOUGHT TO BE POLLUTION, BUT THIS FRAGILE ECOSYSTEM IS EASILY DAMAGED AND IS AT RISK FROM NUMEROUS FACTORS, INCLUDING TOURISM AND GLOBAL WARMING.

REEF ENCOUNTERS

Islanders from the Torres Strait and Aborigines from Australia have been fishing around the Barrier Reef for more than 60,000 years. They are now known as the Traditional Owners of the Great Barrier Reef, and work to conserve the region's biodiversity, and its cultural history. Scientists began studying the reef in the 18th century, after the ship of British explorer James Cook ran aground on the coral.

▲ Nautiluses have scarcely changed in millions of years, and are considered to be living fossils.

Rain forest of the sea

A journey under the sea reveals another magical side to the reef: in the silence of the turquoise waters an underwater carnival of colors is revealed. The reef provides a habitat for an enormous range of wildlife, producing an astonishing level of biodiversity. Schools of tiny silvery fish dart between the weirdly shaped corals, and on their rocky surfaces there are pink mollusks, blue starfish, purple anemones, transparent shrimps, and garish worms. Large predators, such as sharks and squid, venture close to shore to feed and breed. The coral provides plenty of hiding places.

◄ Sweetlips fish undergo incredible color transformations as they age, often becoming less colorful but more boldly patterned.

▼ Jellyfish are closely related to the coral polyps that build the reef. They move with a pulsing rhythm and catch animals in their stinging tentacles.

Valley of THE MOON

Captivatingly beautiful in its austerity, Wadi Rum has inspired many writers to attempt to describe the maze of skyscraper-like monoliths that rise from the desert sand. Part of this landscape's spectacular impact comes from the play of light on the rocks, and the life-giving effect of water in an arid land.

Vast valleys

The Wadi Rum valley cuts through south Jordan. Layers of beige, orange, red, and gray sedimentary sandstones rest upon an ancient layer of granite that is more than 2 billion years old. The tectonic events that continue to shape the Great Rift Valley have tilted and fractured the sandstones, which have been eroded by wind and rain into stone sculptures, arches, and canyons.

▼ One of the rock formations in Wadi Rum was named after T. E. Lawrence's book *The Seven Pillars of Wisdom*—although the seven pillars in the book have no connection with Wadi Rum.

◀▼ Desert scenes in the 1962 movie, *Lawrence of Arabia*, were shot in Wadi Rum, which was the original location of much of the historical action.

Lawrence of Arabia

Wadi Rum was an important site during World War I (1914–1918) when the Arabs were in revolt against the Ottomans. Prince Faisal Bin Hussein and British soldier T. E. Lawrence (known as Lawrence of Arabia) made their base here.

COLUMBIA PICTURES presents THE SAM SPIEGEL · DAVID LEAN Production of

LAWRENCE OF ARABIA

WINNER OF **7** ACADEMY AWARDS

ALEC GUINNESS · ANTHONY QUINN · JACK HAWKINS · JOS.
ANTHONY QUAYLE · CLAUDE RAINS · ARTHUR KENNEDY
OMAR SHARIF as 'ALI' introducing PETER O'TOOLE as 'LAWRENCE'
A HORIZON BRITISH PRODUCTION IN TECHNICOLOR

Spring awakening

After the winter rains, Wadi Rum's natural springs swell, causing the desert to explode with life. Plants such as poppies and black irises bloom in the usually barren ground, and hardy animals such as snakes, ibex, gray wolves, and foxes also survive in the harsh landscape.

▼ The desert lark is one of more than 100 bird species that have been recorded at Wadi Rum.

▶ Crocuses rest as corms during dry periods, but grow and flower after rainfall.

▼ The tectonic events that continue to shape the Rift Valley have tilted and fractured the sandstones of Wadi Rum. They have been eroded by wind, rain, and flash floods into red cliffs and deep canyons.

A POPULAR MOVIE LOCATION, WADI RUM WAS USED TO PORTRAY THE SURFACE OF MARS IN "RED PLANET" (2000) AND EGYPT IN "TRANSFORMERS: REVENGE OF THE FALLEN" (2009).

▼ Jordan's Desert Patrol still sends its famous Camel Corps to police areas of the Wadi Rum where even Land Rovers cannot reach.

Intrepid travelers

People have been traveling through this desert for millennia. Many of them have left archeological evidence that hints at the region's rich history, from flint axes and prehistoric rock carvings to the remains of a 2,000-year-old temple built by Nabataean people. Today, tribal Bedouins still herd their goats through the canyons, camping in goat-hair tents when following their traditional nomadic lifestyle.

ICE
Mountains

In Europe, the Alps **form** a vast mountain barrier. **They** dominate the continent, shaping **its** land and even affecting its culture **and** history. Although they are **situated** in a temperate region, **the Alps** endure lashing ice storms **in winter and the** peaks stay snowy **all year** round.

Pyramid peak

With its steep, angular peak the Matterhorn is Europe's iconic mountain—easy to recognize and with a dangerous reputation. Despite its height, the Matterhorn's four faces are virtually snowless because of their steepness. The first ascent of the mountain took place in 1865, with a loss of four lives. Since then, many hundreds more climbers have died scaling its heights, and the Matterhorn still has one of the highest death rates in the world.

▲ The Matterhorn straddles the border between Switzerland and Italy and is 14,693 ft (4,478 m) tall. Italians call it *Monte Cervino*. It requires great technical skill to climb because the rock is unstable, and variable weather conditions prevail.

As the glacier grinds onward, the combination of the great weight of ice and the rocks inside it scours the landscape.

Making mountains

The Alps are 650 mi (about 1,050 km) long and up to 120 mi (about 200 km) wide. Several Alpine mountains are more than 13,000 ft (4,000 m) tall, and the tallest is Mont Blanc in France. The range began to form about 90 million years ago when two tectonic plates began to converge. The plates crushed and folded the layers of rock between them, forcing them into mountains and valleys, which have been eroded and shaped by glaciation in the last two million years.

Great glaciers

The Aletsch Glacier is an enormous frozen river of ice moving slowly southward from Alpine peaks toward the Rhône Valley. Although it is moving downhill because of gravity, the glacier's front is retreating because it melts as it comes down into warmer air. Water flowing under the ice causes the glacier to deposit its cargo of rocks, creating sediments known as moraines. The Aletsch is Europe's largest valley glacier, measuring 16 mi (25 km), although it has retreated about 2 mi (3 km) in the last 150 years.

The flowers in an Alpine meadow are usually small and low-growing to minimize damage from winds and frosts. They help to create stunning summer panoramas, with backdrops of snow-tipped mountains.

Alpine meadows

Even mighty mountains are not strong enough to withstand the weather. Over millions of years rain, ice, wind, and snow eroded the Alpine rocks, gradually turning them, with organic debris, into soil that can support meadows. The high Alpine meadows are relatively inaccessible, and are now some of Europe's least spoiled habitats. Seemingly fragile plants can survive under snow during winter, then burst into life when the snow melts, creating a dazzling carpet of flowers.

WILDLIFE
Hideaway

The island of Madagascar is a place like no other—literally. It broke away from Africa 150–180 million years ago and now exists as a mini-continent of natural wonders with a bewilderingly diverse range of landscapes and wildlife.

MASSIVE MASSIF

An enormous sheer rock face draws adventurers to central Madagascar. Known as the Tsaranoro Massif, the 2,600-ft (800-m) granite cliff is almost vertical, making it an interesting challenge for climbers, and an awesome spot for the bravest paragliders and base jumpers.

▲ With nowhere to camp out, climbers aim to climb the granite cliffs of Tsaranoro in just one day. The rock faces are solid without cracks, so climbers drill bolts into the cliff to ascend new routes.

SPLITTING UP

At 226,662 sq mi (587,051 sq km) in area, Madagascar is Earth's fourth largest island but it was once part of a giant landmass called Gondwana. Around 180 million years ago a chunk of eastern Gondwana began to move away from Africa. More separations followed, forming Antarctica, India, Australia, and Madagascar.

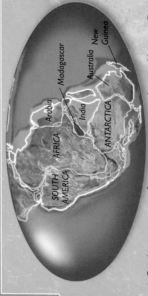

SOUTH AMERICA · AFRICA · Arabia · India · Madagascar · Australia · New Guinea · ANTARCTICA

▲ Gondwana was one of two supercontinents that would eventually split into smaller landmasses. It contained most of the landmasses that are in today's Southern Hemisphere, including Madagascar (red).

MAD

TREASURE TROVES

Separated from the rest of the world, Madagascar embarked on its own evolutionary journey, and most of the species of animals and plants found here live nowhere else. Although much of Madagascar's rain forest has been felled, the remaining areas still harbor 8,000 species of endemic plants, more than 1,000 types of spider, and about 300 species of frog.

▼ Watery habitats are home to many amphibians and fish.

LEMURS ALL ALONE

The first mammals arrived about 60 million years ago, long after the island had been formed. It is thought they arrived on rafts of floating vegetation, and their evolutionary progress continued down a different path to those they had left behind. About 40 species of lemurs, a type of primate with large eyes and foxlike faces, evolved here.

▲ Brown lemurs rarely leave the forest canopy, and feed on fruit, leaves, tree sap, and bugs.

TSINGY LANDS

Parts of Madagascar are virtually impenetrable, where razor-sharp pyramids of rock emerge from the ground. The rocks are so closely packed together it is difficult to find a path between them. They are known as "tsingy" locally, because they make a bell-like sound when struck.

▼ The tsingy peaks were molded by the chemical reaction between rainwater and limestone.

UPSIDE-DOWN TREES

Peculiar baobabs are the iconic trees of the island. Their swollen trunks hold huge stores of water to help the plants get through the dry season, and some baobabs have lived for more than 1,000 years. Lemurs and giant moths suck nectar from their flowers. There are eight species of baobab, and six of them live only on Madagascar.

▼ The Avenue of the Baobabs was once surrounded by lush forest.

frozen Kingdom

Carved by glaciers and exposed to some of Earth's most menacing weather, Svalbard is home to one of the planet's last great wildernesses. This collection of islands lies inside the Arctic Circle and encounters extraordinary phenomena, including the Northern Lights.

▲ Aurorae occur at heights of 50–600 mi (80–1000 km) above Earth, and these silent, flickering displays can be any combination of green, yellow, blue, and red.

Glacier on the move

About 80 percent of Spitsbergen, the main island in Svalbard, is covered by glaciers. One of the most famous of these is Kongsvegen. This mighty river of ice covers about 40 sq mi (105 sq km) and has a length of about 12 mi (20 km). As its low-lying tip, or terminus, reaches the sea, enormous chunks of ice break off to form icebergs.

▲ The molecular structure of ice is less dense than that of liquid water. This means that icebergs can float in seas and rivers.

Archipelago of ice

Spitsbergen's snowcapped Tre-Kroner Mountains give way to a huge inlet called Kongsfjorden, where ice-cold Arctic waters meet the warmer Atlantic Ocean. Enormous icebergs litter the entrance of the fjord, but the warmer waters entice an unexpected array of wildlife to the area, from fulmars to black-legged kittiwakes. In summer, up to three million birds flock to Svalbard, where they are able to feed for 24 hours when the midnight Sun lights up the land, even during the dead of night.

▲ As Kongsvegen reaches the sea it extends into the Kongsfjorden (a fjord) and icebergs (in the foreground) break away.

Northern Lights

Under a still, cold winter's sky, one of the most extraordinary reminders of the planet's place in a bigger Universe is often on view. The Northern Lights, or *Aurora Borealis*, are fleeting visible displays of electrical and magnetic forces. Sheets of light move across the star-studded sky, and their sweeping spectral colors indicate that electric particles from solar winds are splitting oxygen and nitrogen-based molecules in the atmosphere.

IN 1925, EXPLORER ROALD AMUNDSEN ATTEMPTED TO FLY FROM SVALBARD TO THE NORTH POLE IN A DORNIER WAL FLYING BOAT—AND FAILED.

Sparkling snowbows

When sunlight hits rain it can trigger a rainbow, and when it hits flakes of falling snow, a rare sight—the snowbow—may result. Ice crystals in snow bend, or refract, light rays causing them to separate into their constituent rainbow colors.

▶ Snowbows are rare phenomena because they only form in conditions of bright sunlight and light snow.

▼ Polar bears take what they can find. This predator is scavenging on the remains of a fin whale.

Arctic hunters

Svalbard is shared by humans and other mammals that are better equipped to withstand the extreme weather. Polar bears are one of the few mammals that will actively hunt humans, although they usually feed on seals instead. They roam over huge areas in Svalbard, and are as adept at swimming as they are at walking over vast expanses of ice.

Big Island's FIRE

Many of Earth's most awesome features and processes lie hidden beneath its surface. At volcanic hotspots, however, the majestic power of our planet is on view, and there are few better places to witness it than in Hawaii.

HAWAII'S BIG ISLAND

According to Native Hawaiian mythology, when Pele—the goddess of volcanoes—is angry she stamps her feet, causing earthquakes, and starts volcanic eruptions with a shake of her magic stick. If the myth is true, Pele must be furious with Hawaii's Big Island—this is a record-breaking volcanic hotspot without equal on Earth.

MAUNA LOA

- The world's largest active volcano.
- Dome is 64 miles (103 km) across.
- One of the biggest single mountains in the world.
- In 1950, a lava flow from a single fissure devastated a nearby village.

Aloha Mauna Loa

Mauna Loa's great mass covers more than half of Hawaii's Big Island. Its first well-documented eruption occurred in 1843 and Mauna Loa has erupted more than 30 times since. By radiocarbon-dating the lava, scientists have discovered that the first eruption occurred up to one million years ago—and it is almost certain that it will erupt again.

▼ Lava fountains on Mauna Loa spew out from fissures during an eruption. The lava is almost fluid, so it flows easily.

▼ Kea's often snow-capped dome has numerous cinder cones—deposits that build up around volcanic vents.

MAUNA KEA

- 5.6 mi (9 km) in height from its base on the ocean floor.
- Dome is 30 mi (50 km) across.
- The world's largest astronomical observatory is sited on its slopes.

Colossal Kea

The islands of Hawaii have been developing over the last five million years—the result of volcanoes forming as the Pacific tectonic plate passes over a hotspot in Earth's mantle layer. Mauna Kea, which is now dormant, began erupting on the seafloor about 800,000 years ago and if it is measured from this base Kea is actually taller than Mount Everest. Its last eruption occurred 4,500 years ago but volcanologists believe it may be spurred into action again.

◀ Aside from its enormous volcanoes, Big Island also has many climate zones, from jungles to snow-topped mountains.

FIREFIGHTERS

Volcanologists conduct crucial work, often putting their lives at risk to gather information about volcanic activity. They are still unable to accurately predict earthquakes and volcanoes, but collecting data such as changes in temperature, gases, lava flows, and seismic activity help to build accurate pictures of precursors to major tectonic events.

KILAUEA

- The world's most active volcano.
- Spews, on average, 130,000 gal (around 492,000 l) of lava every minute.
- Repeated explosive eruptions make it one of the most dangerous volcanoes on Earth.

▼ Black, burning lava from Kilauea spews into the sea, below a hardened lava crust.

Constant eruption

The sights, sounds, and smells of an active volcano smother the senses. Pungent gases, ash, and lava have been erupting from one of the cinder cones (called Pu`u Ō) of Kilauea since 1983. It may be a young shield volcano, with most of its structure still below sea level, but Kilauea has wreaked devastation on its environment, destroying ancient archeological sites, villages, and rain forest.

EMERALD Scene

In 3,000 places on Mexico's Yucatán Peninsula the Sun's warming rays pass through pools or shafts known as cenotes. These holes in the landscape are entrance points to a spectacular underworld that features flooded caverns, ancient Mayan ceremonial altars, and blind fish.

▶ Lush tropical vegetation surrounds Yucatán's cenotes, thanks to a plentiful supply of groundwater in the region.

Sun-filled basins

In Yucatán, most of these caverns contain pools of sparkling groundwater that is incredibly clean, having been filtered by its passage through the limestone. In some places, shafts of light reach down into the caverns, and plants are able to grow. Deep pools of water are home to species of blind fish, and colonies of bats roost along dark stone ledges.

◀ Belize slider turtles feed on vegetation in cenotes, but can clamber out to bask in the sunlight.

The Place of Fear

Few rivers run across the land above this subterranean structure, as all the water flows down holes and into the caverns beneath, in some instances creating cenotes. These wells had great meaning to the Mayans who lived here—they were seen as gateways to the underworld, known as *Xibalba*, or the "Place of Fear." Some cenotes were used as water sources, but others were used for the purpose of sacrifice, and people were thrown into the pools to appease the god of rain.

▲ This ancient skull was found in a cenote, and was possibly that of a human sacrifice victim.

Big impact

The surrounding rock was once part of a giant limestone plain, which was probably damaged by the Chicxulub meteorite that fell here around 65 million years ago, sparking the demise of the dinosaurs. The rock plateau has been further weakened and dissolved by rainwater. Over time, small caves and tunnels have collapsed, creating enormous caverns.

VISION IS OF NO USE TO LITTLE DAMA FISH LIVING IN DARK CENOTES, SO OVER TIME THEY HAVE LOST THEIR EYES.

Flower caves

About 300 mi (500 km) of the caves and watery tunnels have been mapped so far. The largest caves at Yucatán are called Loltun Caves, and their name derives from the Mayan words for "stone flower." Stalactites in these caves create a bell-like chime when struck, and archeological finds suggest that the caves were first inhabited 7,000 years ago.

◄ The limestone structures in the Gran Cenote are often compared to a tiny city of skyscrapers.

WONDER
No More

We are changing **our** planet at a rate that **has** only been equalled in **the past** by cataclysmic events, **such** as massive meteorite **impacts** and supervolcano **eruptions.** Only future **generations** will fully comprehend **the damage** we are doing to **some of** Earth's most awesome **places.**

▼ Parts of Virunga National Park have been devastated by the clearing of land for farming using "slash-and-burn."

War-torn wilderness

Despite suffering a century of poaching and years of war, the small population of mountain gorillas in Virunga National Park, in the Democratic Republic of the Congo, clings to life. However, the habitat is under relentless pressure from the growing human population, and large areas of forest have been destroyed.

▶ The Virunga National Park is the oldest reserve in Africa and is home to around 100 mountain gorillas.

▼ Varieties of coral create a carpet of colors. Their unusual shapes give rise to common names, such as brain, lettuce, fan, and star coral.

Watery grave

The corals of Belize have been described as the most outstanding barrier reef in the Northern Hemisphere and a significant habitat for endangered species, such as marine turtles, manatees, and American marine crocodiles.

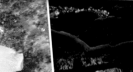

▲ Belize corals are being bleached (killed) by a combination of pollution and rising temperatures.

Dead and gone

The Dead Sea has been shrinking for 10,000 years, but in just 25 years its area has diminished by one fifth. As more water is extracted from the River Jordan, less reaches the Dead Sea. Water is also removed for salt production.

▼ The Dead Sea is a landlocked hypersaline lake between Israel and Jordan.

▼ A pumping station removes water from the Dead Sea to evaporation pools, so salts can be extracted.

◄ Slash pines growing in the freshwater areas of Florida create a habitat for birds and small mammals. The timber is also of commercial use.

Everglades forever?

For the last 70 years, developers have been draining Florida's Everglades swamps to build on the reclaimed land, and water has been diverted from the swamps to supply agriculture and urban areas. The effects have been described as environmental ruin.

▲ Housing developments on the Everglades replace precious habitats and destroy entire ecosystems.

Earth's POWER

From tornadoes that tear up the land to earthquakes that burn it to cinders, find out about the fierce natural forces that wreak havoc on our planet.

Early Eruptions	116
Blowing its Top	118
Angry Oceans	120
Vanishing Coasts	122
Sand Blasted	124
Fire! Fire!	126
Tsunami!	128
Flash! Boom!	130
Winds of Destruction	132
Mega Monsoons	134
Huge Holes	136
Falling Down	138
Typhoon Terror	140
Haiti Quake	142
Twister Central	144
Too Much Water	146
Storm of the Century	148

◀ Lightning strikes as a gigantic supercell storm looms over South Dakota, U.S., creating an eerily dramatic display.

Early ERUPTIONS

A large volcanic eruption is massive, sudden, and savage. It shakes the ground, raining molten lava and ash over a vast area. Today, such an eruption only occurs every 10 or 20 years. But just after Earth formed, much of the world was in volcanic turmoil.

4.54 billion years ago
Earth forms

4.52 billion years ago
Collision with space body knocks out a chunk—the Moon

4.5 billion years ago
Volcanoes begin erupting

▼ Earth formed as small fragments of rock stuck together. The protoplanet grew quickly in size and also formed an atmosphere.

◄ Early planets, called protoplanets, formed when their gravitational forces collected surrounding rock and dust.

From dust we came

Long ago, a supernova exploded causing a shockwave that disturbed a giant dust-gas cloud. This cloud started to spin, then condensed, compressing into lumps. The central bulge became the fiery Sun and the outer chunks formed planets. By 4.5 billion years ago, the solar system had formed.

▼ Fierce rainstorms lasted for thousands of years, as floods and giant waves shaped the early land.

EARTH'S EARLY ATMOSPHERE CONTAINED MANY DEADLY GASES.

Boiling rocks

Early Earth was a hellish place. As gases and dust collapsed under the pressure of their own increasing gravity, they became hot rocks. Volcanoes covered huge areas and erupted for millions of years. Poisonous fumes and ashes spurted from the surface, and glowing rivers of rock flooded from cracks and vents. The enormous heat and toxic atmosphere meant that no life could survive.

Violent birth

Chunks of matter circling the Sun attracted other lumps and grew into several protoplanets, one being Earth. It was a time of colossal impacts as space debris knocked these bodies around, added to them, or smashed lumps out of them. As the protoplanets rotated, they took on spherical (ball-like) shapes.

Sea fury

As the planet cooled, volcanic vapors condensed into liquid water. More water may have formed during the Late Heavy Bombardment, a time of repeated meteorite and asteroid smashes that vaporized on impact. The new water trickled down rocky slopes and pooled as seas and oceans. It was still hot, and the rocks steamed. Slowly the savage conditions subsided and temperatures calmed. In water, early microbes appeared. The era of life began.

117

BLOWING its Top

Some volcanoes ooze and spit every day. Others have months or years between bursts. Mount St. Helens had been dormant for many years before it erupted in March 1980, wreaking havoc on the U.S. state of Washington and the 11 surrounding states. But what was it like to be there?

The northern bulge developed over three weeks and rose by 450 ft (135 m).

March 20

Our geological team arrived near Mount St. Helens after a 90-mi (145-km) trip south from Seattle. Reports of small tremors for several days now. Two days ago a Richter 4.1 'quake shook the flank. After more than 120 years, dormant "Helen" is waking up.

The team collected vapor samples from vents to analyze for sulfur dioxide and other component gases.

March 27

We've set up seismometers, theodolites, and other equipment. Two huge geyserlike spurts of steam, ash, vapor, and rock erupted with fearsome noise. The existing summit crater has developed a smaller parasitic crater 250 ft (76 m) across. Further preshocks shake the area.

March 30

Small tremors occur every few minutes. Another parasitic crater has appeared. Outgassings—trapped gas released from the ground—ignited by lava brighten the night sky. A storm produced massive lightning bolts that flickered through ash clouds.

April 29

Triangulation readings using slope angles show the north side of the mountain bulges by 250 ft (76 m) and grows 6 ft (2 m) every day, due to internal pressure from rising magma. Hundreds of tremors daily.

March 1980

Tuesday	Wednesday	Thursday	Friday	Saturday
				1
4	5	6	7	8
11	12	13	14	15
18	19	20 ✱	21	22
25	26 ✱	27	28	29
31				

May 23

It's five days after the primary eruption, heard more than 200 mi (320 km) away. Readings show the mountain is 1,300 ft (400 m) lower. Aircraft monitoring indicates the ash cloud rose to 10,000 ft (3,000 m), visible for hundreds of miles. Ash is falling 2,000 mi (3,200 km) away.

Blasted by the volcano's force, stripped logs lie like matchsticks on nearby Spirit Lake, which rose by 200 ft (60 m).

BREAKING NEWS

MAY 18, 1980: MOUNT ST. HELENS ERUPTS!

Just after 8.30 p.m. seismometers almost went off the scale. Helens' north side blasted apart. A massive outpouring of lava, like a gigantic landslide, traveled at 150 mph (240 km/h) and left a path of slurry, rocks, and debris more than 17 mi (27 km) long. Seismic activity peaked at 3 pm. With pressure released, pyroclastic flows—superheated clouds of ash, rock particles, and gases—scorched an area 25 mi (40 km) wide and 20 mi (32 km) long. Glaciers melted and lahars (large mudflows) mixed in, flowing for almost 50 mi (80 km).

The Daily News

HELENS' AFTERMATH

57 deaths!

200 homes and buildings destroyed!

180 mi (290 km) of roads gone!

More than 250 sq mi (650 sq km) burned to cinders!

BLANKETS OF ASH COVER THE SURFACE—HOW ARE YOU GETTING AROUND?

Yet in weeks plants sprouted, and in months many animals were back!

ANGRY Oceans

Water is heavy—15 bathtubs of water weigh as much as a family saloon car. On the move, this water has immense destructive power. Seawater is always moving as tides, currents, whirlpools, waterspouts, and storm surges.

▼ In the Bay of Fundy, Canada, the tidal range exceeds 59 ft (18 m). At low tide, fishing boats are grounded. Only five hours later, at high tide, water fills the harbor.

River wave

Tidal bores or "traveling waves" need a tidal range—the difference between high and low tide—of more than 20 ft (6 m). This allows the rising water to funnel into a narrow, shallow river and push against the flow. The tallest bore in the world is on Qiantang River, China. It's 30 ft (9 m) high and races along at 25 mph (40 km/h). The 7-ft (2-m) bore on England's Severn River benefits from a huge tidal range of almost 50 ft (15 m).

◄ March 2010's Severn bore attracted surfers from around the world.

Relentless tides

The rise and fall of the tides comes from the interplay of gravity from the Moon and Sun, combined with Earth's 24-hour spin. Tidal range increases where water piles up in long bays or estuaries. Both Canada's Bay of Fundy and Ungava Bay have extreme tidal ranges, more than 53 ft (16 m)—enough to cover a four-story building.

WATERSPOUTS—TORNADOES OVER WATER—CAN BE UP TO 330 FT (100 M) ACROSS AND 5,000 FT (1,500 M) TALL, WITH WINDS UP TO 250 FT/S (76 M/S).

IN A SWIRL

Tides and currents create fierce ocean whirlpools. When adjacent tidal waters flow at different speeds or in opposite directions, they "rub edges," and spin. Massive whirlpools, or maelstroms, are 150 ft (46 m) across with waves curling 3 ft (one meter) tall. Despite legend, there is little downward flow, so whirlpools do not sink ships.

▼ Japan's 2011 tsunami caused major whirlpools, hundreds of feet wide, off the coast.

THE FLOW OF WATER IN THE SALTSTRAUMEN MAELSTROM, NORWAY, PEAKS AT 40 MPH (64 KM/H)

Water surge

Storms can generate such strong winds along low coasts, they pile up seawater and blow it onto the land. When water is funneled into a bay, the effects are extreme. In 1899, Tropical Cyclone Mahina's winds drove a surge of water 45 ft (14 m) tall onto Bathurst Bay, northeast Australia. More than 300 people died. Seawater flooded the land, leaving behind salt that destroyed the land's ability to grow plants for many years.

▼ In 2007, storm surges threatened strong sea defenses in Scheveningen, the Netherlands.

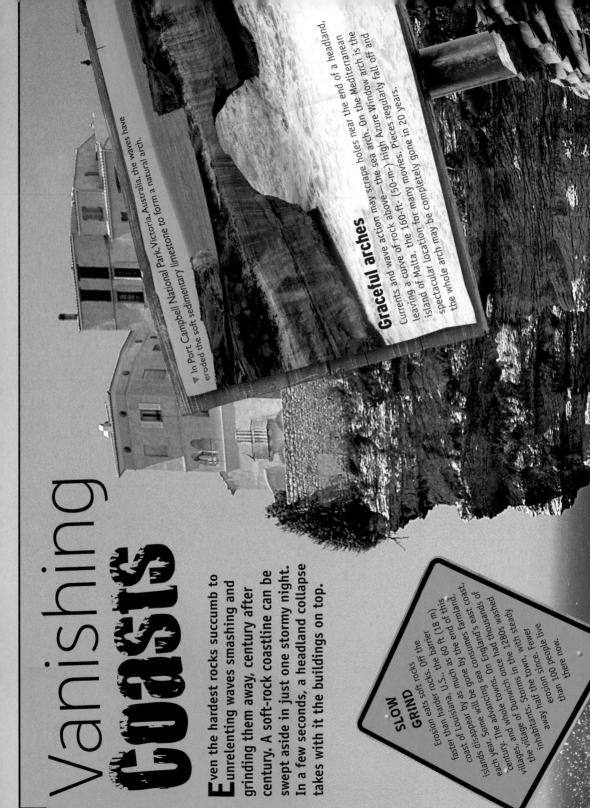

Vanishing coasts

Even the hardest rocks succumb to unrelenting waves smashing and grinding them away, century after century. A soft-rock coastline can be swept aside in just one stormy night. In a few seconds, a headland collapse takes with it the buildings on top.

▼ In Port Campbell National Park, Victoria, Australia, the waves have eroded the soft sedimentary limestone to form a natural arch.

Graceful arches

Currents and wave action may scrape holes near the end of a headland, leaving a curve of rock above—the sea arch. On the Mediterranean island of Malta, the 160-ft- (50-m-) high Azure Window is the spectacular location for many movies. Pieces regularly fall off and the whole arch may be completely gone in 20 years.

SLOW GRIND

Erosion eats soft rocks. Off the coast of Louisiana, U.S., the barrier islands disappear by as much as 60 ft (18 m) faster than harder rocks. Some will be gone by the end of this century. The advancing sea consumes England's east coast, and whole towns. On thousands of each year. The once had thousands washed villages, and 1280s steady inhabitants. Dunwich the town, with half the Storms in with Fewer away erosion since. people live than 100 there now.

Land vs. sea

Coastal erosion is the wearing away of land by wind, tides, and waves. The severity of erosion depends on a number of factors—type and hardness of the rock, shoreline height and contours, prevailing wind speed, angle of water currents, and the likelihood of storms. One of the main problems is undercutting, where waves erode tall land at sea level, leaving the rock above ready to collapse.

▲ Large storm waves pick up sand, pebbles, and boulders and hurl them at the rock face, slowly undercutting a cliff in Corsica, France.

Disappearing islands

Islands are vanishing for a number of reasons. The islet of Surtsey, near Iceland, appeared when a submerged volcano poked above the waves in 1963. It grew until 1967, and now erosion is causing it to shrink. Some islands are sinking because the tectonic plates—giant curved slabs of rock that form Earth's crust—are gradually descending into Earth's mantle. Increasingly a major culprit is global warming, which expands water in the oceans, and also causes icy regions to melt and therefore sea levels to rise.

▲ Coastal erosion washes away sand and soil where trees once grew, uprooting and killing them.

IN NOVEMBER 2010, HURRICANE TOMAS STRUCK THE CARIBBEAN. CLIFF COLLAPSES AT SOUFRIÈRE, ST. LUCIA, MADE MORE THAN 5,000 PEOPLE HOMELESS.

Sand BLASTED

It begins as a vague haze on the horizon. The advancing wall of boiling sand and dust never seems to come into focus, but gets bigger and roars louder. Then suddenly—brown-out. You can hardly see your hands, but you don't want to look. The whipping particles sting your eyes, flay your ears, assault your nostrils, and choke your throat. Time to take cover.

▼ In 2009, red outback soil blew into Sydney, Australia, forcing people indoors and a transport shutdown.

Rapid spread

A haboob is a small, powerful, concentrated dust storm caused by a clustered mass of cool, heavy air moving along within a region of warm air. It occurs when storm clouds break up and sink to the ground as downbursts, fragmenting into several horizontal flows. Haboobs affect dry places such as the Sahara desert, Middle East, Central Australia, and southwest North America. They happen fast and their winds reach 60 mph (96 km/h), but usually pass in a few minutes.

Dusty city

In southwest U.S., sandstorms and dust storms are common in summer when a wind shift brings moisture-laden subtropical air from the south. This triggers thunderstorms with downbursts that kick up the desert's thin soil. Phoenix, Arizona, is regularly menaced by dusty 60-mph (96-km/h) winds that smother people, traffic, aircraft, and air-conditioners.

▶ Following an especially dry spring, a summer "dusty" rolls in from the parched surrounds to suffocate downtown Phoenix, U.S.

The right ingredients

Sandstorms and dust storms need two ingredients to start. The first is loose dry particles, usually in an arid region with extra weeks of no rain, shrunken rivers, and a lowered groundwater level. The second is updraft winds, generally from a large block of dry, cool air that warms and rises as it moves over hot ground. The winds lift the particles so they bounce along, breaking into smaller, lighter pieces that float more easily.

▶ Satellites track a giant dust storm hundreds of miles wide, stretching from northeast Africa to the Arabian Peninsula.

IN 2012 A SUDDEN DUST STORM IN RIYADH, SAUDI ARABIA, TURNED DAY INTO NIGHT—VEHICLE AND BUILDING LIGHTS CAME ON AT ONLY 4 P.M.

SLOW-MOTION SAVAGERY

Sandstorms and dust storms are part of long-term desertification. In dry regions, overgrazing by farm animals and too many crops using poor agriculture exhaust the soil, turning it dusty. Drought worsens the problem. In North Africa's Sahel, south of the Sahara, there are 100 days of sandstorms each year, and the human-made "desert" advances by up to 5 mi (8 km).

▲ During one of Kenya's regular droughts, farm workers flee as a dust storm sweeps past. The livestock are malnourished and farms struggle to survive.

Cover up!

When a sandstorm warning goes out, people prepare fast. The wind drives tiny grains through the smallest gaps and cracks, so that one small draft leaves everything inside coated with fine dust. Cover must be sought. Valuable items such as cars, tractors, wells, and irrigation vents are protected; and doors, shutters, windows, and other openings are closed and sealed.

▶ In the city of Turpan, northwest China, residents continue with their day while wearing masks to avoid inhaling the dust.

Fire! Fire!

An uncontrollable fire breaks out in the countryside, devouring the vegetation. A wildfire has begun. Wildfires can be the result of natural causes—lightning strikes, volcanic lava and ash, sparks from rockfalls, and even the Sun's rays focused through natural clear crystals. Nowadays, human error is also a major factor.

◀ On East Africa's vast grasslands, animals such as gazelles are used to outrunning the fast-approaching bushfires.

▲ To make a firebreak, firefighters pour flaming fuel from driptorches on the ground.

Part of nature

Wildfires are natural seasonal events in regions such as the East African savanna, American prairie, and Central Australian bush. Each year the dry period breaks as thunderstorms sweep in. Lightning torches the tinder-dry grass and scrub, and winds fan the flames. The flare-ups are rapid and fierce, but they soon fade as the rainy season gets underway.

Fighting fire

Modern firefighting has many methods to tackle big blazes. Vegetation can be prehosed to make it damp and less likely to catch. In areas at regular risk, firefighters often light small-scale burns to create open gaps called firebreaks. Finally, helicopters and "super-scooper" planes drop water to douse the flames.

▼ In Bunyip State Park, near Melbourne, Australia, the fire service monitors the spread of an enormous fire, with smoke filling the sky.

BLACK SATURDAY

One of Australia's worst tragedies began on February 7, 2009. In the southern state of Victoria, after two dry months, the temperature soared above 110°F (43°C) and winds gusted at 60 mph (96 km/h). More than 400 bushfires flared up, with causes ranging from sparking power lines to careless campfires. More fires broke out over the following three weeks. The final toll was 173 human deaths, dozens of towns destroyed, and huge areas of land scorched.

▼ Just three months after Australia's "Black Saturday," tree ferns in the hills of Victoria state were already extending their delicate new fronds.

▼ Firefighters nervously watch the wind direction in a raging central California forest fire.

Whipped by wind

High winds fan flames and make a fire spread at speeds of 15 mph (24 km/h) or more. Steady wind direction gives firefighters a chance to predict the burn area and make preparations. Sudden wind changes can alter the fire's route, trapping people and vehicles. In 2012, six firefighters died when a blaze near Carahue, Southern Chile, changed direction.

Black to green

Plants and animals cope well with natural wildfires. Trees have thick bark, grass roots are safe underground, and herbs make heat-resistant seeds that germinate after scorching. Animals hide underground, take flight, or flee. As the flames die down, shoots sprout up. In a few weeks, the blackened carpet turns green and life returns.

NEWS

TSUNAMI!

PETER JONES Tohoku, Japan LIVE

At 2:46 p.m. local time, a colossal earthquake shook Tohoku, the northern region of Japan's main island, Honshu. Giant waves are forecast to hit the closest shoreline within 30 minutes. Depending on seabed and coastal contours, some waves can reach 120 ft (35 m) high and surge more than 6 mi (10 km) inland. They are likely to flood huge areas of coastline.

THE CAUSE

Tsunami swell

Wave hits land

Earthquake's focus

Tectonic plates moving one beneath another

The earthquake that triggered the tsunami was a megathrust event—two tectonic plates forming Earth's crust slipped, forcing one above the other. Scientists estimate its origin as 41 mi (66 km) east of Tohoku's coast and 20 mi (32 km) below the surface. The event lasted for six minutes and caused parts of the seabed to shift sideways by 160 ft (50 m) and rise up 20 ft (6 m). This shift pushed the water above, setting off the tsunami.

A FEW HOURS LATER

The rushing water carried everything in its path. Boats, cars, trucks, and trains were swept along like toys. Houses, offices, and factories were smashed to pieces in seconds. Hundreds of miles of roads, railroad lines, drainage systems, and other infrastructure were destroyed.

THREE DAYS LATER

An explosion occured at the Fukushima Nuclear Power Plant on the coast hit by flooding. The earthquake's tremors triggered auto-shutdown. However, the floods immobilized the reactor's cooling system, causing potential nuclear meltdown. People within 12 mi (20 km) were immediately evacuated.

Flash!

Severe thunderstorms are some of Earth's most vicious events. Every second around the world, more than 2,000 places are under towering clouds, suffering torrential rain, huge hailstones, and violent winds. Thunderstorms cause great damage and destruction, leaving behind a shattered landscape.

The mothership

The biggest thunderstorms come from massive atmospheric features called supercells, which can be 50 mi (80 km) across and 12 mi (20 km) high. They form where warm air collides with cold air. Winds make the warm air rise and spin, gradually tilting upright with swirling updrafts inside.

▶ A storm hit South Dakota on July 23, 2010, bringing with it a giant supercell that poured record-breaking hailstones onto the area. The hailstones measured 8 in (20 cm) in diameter.

Ups and downs

As it rises, water vapor cools, causing it to condense and even freeze. During a thunderstorm, this produces towering cumulonimbus "anvil" clouds. Inside the clouds, water droplets are moved around in a cycle—rising, combining, falling, and then rising again. Eventually these icy balls may cause a heavy fall of hail or snow.

▼ A space station view 250 mi (400 km) high shows giant cumulonimbus over West Africa. The cloud flattened and spread out as it hit a natural barrier along the base of the stratosphere.

Stones of ice

Water vapor is blown to the top of a thunderstorm by updrafts of more than 100 mph (160 km/h). Here the temperature is many degrees below freezing. The drops eventually fall and thaw, merging together before being caught in an updraft again. This is how hailstones grow. The biggest exceed 8 in (20 cm) and weigh up to 2 lb (one kg).

▼ In June 2012, hailstones larger than tennis balls dented and smashed vehicles in Dallas.

Ash and flash

Lightning is caused by a buildup of electrical charges in a cloud. The positive charges are near the cloud's top and the negative are lower down. The difference in charges becomes so great that finally a giant spark leaps to even them out— lightning. This instantly heats the air around it, forming a shock wave that spreads out like a sonic boom—thunder.

▶ Lightning appears in the plume of ash above the Chaiten volcano in southern Chile during the 2008 eruption. Scientists are unsure what causes a volcanic electrical storm.

AN AVERAGE LIGHTNING BOLT...

⚡ has enough electrical energy to power a typical household for one week

⚡ has an electrical "push" of more than one billion volts. Domestic supply is 112–120 v (220–240 v)

⚡ has a temperature of 55,000°F (30,500°C)—eight times hotter than the Sun's surface

⚡ measures 1–2 mi (1.6–3.2 km) in length

⚡ has a flow of electricity, or current, of more than 250,000 amps. A low-energy lightbulb has a current of less than 0.1 amps

Winds of
DESTRUCTION

Many atmospheric events cause the mass movement of air. Extreme winds often whip up as warm air clashes with cold air—resulting in a furious battle that inflicts devastation on the land below and creates havoc for planes in the sky.

DOWNBURSTS MORE THAN 2.5 MI (4 KM) ACROSS ARE KNOWN AS MACROBURSTS; SMALLER ONES ARE KNOWN AS MICROBURSTS.

Straight-line damage

A derecho is a widespread, fast-moving band of damaging straight-line winds and clusters of savage thunderstorms. Winds span more than 250 mi (400 km), persist for at least six hours, and reach a speed of at least 58 mph (93 km/h). Within the derecho are storms, rain, hail, and sudden wind currents called downbursts.

▲ Microbursts occur when air suddenly becomes colder in a thundercloud, causing an air column to move rapidly downward. If the air was wet, the microburst is joined by rainfall.

▲ A squall line—band of severe thunderstorms—can produce a derecho.

▶ Downbursts are extremely dangerous to aircraft because the increased wind speed can cause a pilot to misjudge the landing speed needed.

Cloud base

DEADLY DOWNBURSTS

In certain storm conditions, raindrops evaporate as they fall. This draws in heat from the air, causing it to cool rapidly and become heavier. When there's enough cold air, it suddenly plummets to the ground, and spreads out from its center. Known as downbursts, the winds can exceed 150 mph (240 km/h).

Downdraft

Horizontal vortex

Outflow front

Rainfall

Small but furious

Lasting just a couple of minutes, the ferocious 150-mph (240-km/h) winds of a microburst can cause as much destruction as a tornado—so people can confuse the two. However, there is a key difference between them. A tornado leaves behind a rotating pattern because winds spin around a center that moves along. Microburst winds blow out in straight lines from the center, causing damage in a radial pattern, like wheel spokes.

▼ The buran occurs often in Mongolia, with winds full of snow and ice, making it difficult for workers to get around.

Relentless blizzards

The buran or "blizzard wind" is a regular fierce airflow, usually from the northeast, that scours Central Asia. In summer, it brings duststorms. In winter, it carries blizzards of snow and ice, at temperatures below -20°F (-28°C). A typical buran blows at more than 35 mph (55 km/h) for several hours, and the snow reduces visibility to 300 ft (90 m) or less.

133

Mega monsoons

In South Asia, the fiery sun heats the land and air over it, faster than the ocean. The hot air rises, and cooler, moist air flows in from the sea as the onshore monsoon wind. The monsoon season has arrived—months of Earth's wettest weather.

Looming danger

Monsoons are caused by seasonal changes in the direction of the wind. Warm, moist air blows in from the Indian Ocean toward southern Asian countries such as Pakistan, India, Bangladesh, and Burma. The air rises over the sunbaked land, then condenses as colossal amounts of rain. Heavy rains usually fall from June to September, starting in South Asia and then spreading to Southeast Asia and Australia.

▼ The first sign of the monsoon's arrival is large rainclouds looming on the horizon.

Pakistan suffers

Beginning in late July 2010, the heaviest monsoon rains for decades inundated Pakistan. Intense torrents over hills cascaded to the lowlands, breaking riverbanks and saturating farms, towns, and villages. By mid-August one fifth of the whole nation was flooded, 20 million people were displaced, and nearly 2,000 had died.

▼ People wade through deep water in an attempt to salvage their belongings after torrential rains caused floods in Pakistan in 2010.

IN JULY 2005, MORE THAN 64 IN (163 CM) OF RAIN FELL IN 36 HOURS ON INDIA'S CITY OF MUMBAI—MORE THAN NEW YORK CITY'S YEARLY RAINFALL.

◀ Children play in storm drains as monsoon rains bring relief from intense summer heat.

Coping with the deluge

Monsoons are regular annual events, and generally the land and the people cope. Storm drains, irrigation channels, road conduits, and other infrastructure are designed to handle the deluges. People also watch out for aquatic animals such as crocodiles that get caught in the flowing water.

SO MUCH RAIN

City	Average annual precipitation
Mawsynram, India	467 in (1,187 cm)
Brazzaville, Congo	73 in (185 cm)
Sydney, Australia	48 in (122 cm)
New York City, U.S.	47 in (119 cm)
Rio de Janeiro, Brazil	43 in (110 cm)
Beijing, China	25 in (63 cm)
London, England	24 in (61 cm)
Los Angeles, U.S.	15 in (38 cm)
Riyadh, Saudi Arabia	4 in (10 cm)

Huge HOLES

One minute the ground is there. Next, there's a great hole. Not all sinkholes form this quickly, but they are a regular feature in some landscapes and can also occur where humans have worked underground.

▼ In 2007, a 330-ft- (100-m-) deep hole formed under Guatemala City in Central America. It was caused by sewage water leaking down through loose soil and old volcanic ash.

Look out below!

Sinkholes, swallowholes, and similar openings usually develop in certain kinds of rock such as limestone, dolomite, or sandstone. Underground rivers gradually erode a hidden cavity or cavern. The cavern gets so big that its roof is no longer supported and caves in.

▲ The Daisetta sinkhole reached an estimated 1,300 ft (400 m) across and 200 ft (60 m) deep.

Bigger and bigger

Some sinkholes start small and grow. At Daisetta, in Texas, U.S., a sinkhole appeared in May 2008. It swallowed trees and vehicles and continued to enlarge, at one stage by 20 ft (6 m) per hour, until it reached 600 ft (180 m) across and 150 ft (45 m) deep. It may have resulted from the collapse of a salt dome—a lump of salt, less dense than surrounding rock, that collected under the crust.

SUDDEN SINKHOLE

On February 28, 2013, a 60-ft (18-m) sinkhole opened up under a house in Florida, swallowing a bedroom. One person was killed as the ground crumbled away. Beneath Florida is a system of limestone caverns, eroded by water, causing them to collapse.

▲ After the house in Florida was demolished, the sinkhole was shown to threaten neighboring properties.

THE NOW-FLOODED LITTLE SALT SPRING SINKHOLES, IN FLORIDA, HAVE PRESERVED 6,500-YEAR-OLD HUMAN REMAINS AND A 13,500-YEAR-OLD PREHISTORIC GIANT TORTOISE.

Heavenly pits

"Tiankeng" is Chinese for "heavenly pit" and the name given to sinkholes at least 330 ft (100 m) deep and wide. Xiaozhai Tiankeng is the world's biggest, more than 2,160 ft (660 m) deep, with a mouth 2,030 ft (620 m) wide. Smaller holes appear regularly, such as the one that almost consumed Qingquan primary school in Dachegnqiao, near Changsha, southeast China in June 2010.

▼ The Qingquan hole grew to 500 ft (150 m) wide and 150 ft (45 m) deep, destroying or undermining 30 dwellings.

Falling DOWN

It takes only a small movement to trigger a landslide or avalanche. Without warning, nature lets loose with a sudden, unstoppable mass movement that covers, smashes, and sweeps away everything in its path.

Savage slips

Landslips and landslides have various triggers, such as heavy rain, erosion, earthquakes, or even loose rock. Poor farming and forestry worsen the risks by removing plant cover from the ground. In December 1999, the state of Vargas, Venezuela, was ravaged by a series of landslips and mudslides after receiving 36 in (91 cm) of rain in three days. Up to 30,000 people died and 300,000 were made homeless.

▶ During Tropical Storm Talas in Japan, 2011, a sudden downpour loosened the soil on this steep slope. It was forced downhill, destroying buildings at the bottom.

WATCH FOR FALLEN ROCKS

Snow slide

When heavy snow piles up on a mountain slope, pressure builds until... snow things can instigate the mountain slope, pressure builds until... snow mass movement—new snowfall, snow movement—a kick from a loud sound. The whoosh, a kick from a loud sound. The melting, and even the slope, the fiercer earth tremor, and smother up to 100 mph (160 steeper and traveling at Blons, Austria, two km/h). In 1954 near Blons, Austria, killed the flow, traveling up to 200 people. avalanches in in quick succession killed more than 200 people.

▶ Rescue workers check the forward edge of an avalanche that tumbled down a slope in the ski resort of Hinterstoder, Austria in April 2009.

Death clouds

A pyroclastic flow is an incredibly rapid, surging cloud of gas and particles superheated, often due to its partial collapse from a volcano, often hot 400 mph. As hot as 1,800°F (1,000°C), the flow cascades downhill at speeds of more than everything downhill. It torches and burns everything (640 km/h). It torches and burns everything in its path. During the 1990s in the Caribbean, parts of the island of Montserrat were overwhelmed by pyroclastic flows, lahars, and ashfalls.

▼ The Soufrière Hills Volcano, Montserrat, regularly belches out cloud. This cloud pyroclastic flows. This cloud followed the collapse of a small bulge on the main lava dome.

IN 1902, THE FLOWS OF PYROCLASTIC, ON THE MOUNT PELÉE, ON OF MOUNT ISLAND KILLED UP CARIBBEAN, KILLED UP MARTINIQUE, KILLED UP TO 30,000 PEOPLE.

▲ Remote mountainous areas often suffer after heavy rain. A mudslide near Mianzhu, China, trapped 500 people in their homes.

▼ Areas where roads are cut into the rock along steep hillsides of scree (loose rocky fragments) are commonly hit by rockfalls.

Muddy mayhem

A lahar is a fast, hot mudflow from an erupting volcano. The sudden heat melts glaciers and snowfields. The sudden heat melts soil to form a slurry of debris that mixes with slopes into valleys and canyons. In 1985 the water mixes with lahars following the eruption of Nevado del town of Armero, Colombia, was engulfed by Ruiz volcano. More than 20,000 lives were lost.

Rock block

Rockfalls occur when melting ice and snow liquify soil on steep slopes, allowing boulders to slip. These boulders tumble downhill, crashing into and moving any rocks in their path. Quickly the rockfall gains size and momentum.

TYPHOON TERROR

Thelma's survivors experience the stench of decay at a mass burial in Ormoc City.

Vast rotating swirls of air, usually centered around low-pressure winds spiraling inward, make deadly weather features. They have different names—hurricanes in the Atlantic and east Pacific, cyclones near India, and typhoons in the northwest Pacific, where the islands of the Philippines are often right in their path...

Typhoon Thelma, 1991

The Philippines is used to several typhoons each season. In October 1991, Thelma was not especially powerful, with winds peaking at 50 mph (80 km/h). But it was certainly devastating, causing more than 6,000 deaths. Immense rainfall flooded the land, with some areas receiving more then 20 in (50 cm) in 24 hours. On the central island of Leyte, many people died from drowning and landslides.

Typhoon Parma, 2009

A few days after Typhoon Ketsana hit the central Philippines in October 2009, Parma hurtled across its northern zone. Peak winds registered at more than 110 mph (175 km/h). The authorities ordered controlled opening of several dams, to avoid them overflowing or cracking under pressure—this meant evacuating thousands of homes. Water transport, from fishing boats and ferries to huge cargo ships, was stopped. The total damage topped $6 million (£3.9 million), making it the Philippines' second costliest typhoon ever.

Parma's floods swept through many Philippine towns and cities, such as Santa Cruz.

1979'S TYPHOON TIP WAS 1,400 MI (2,250 KM) ACROSS WITH WINDS REACHING 190 MPH (305 KM/H).

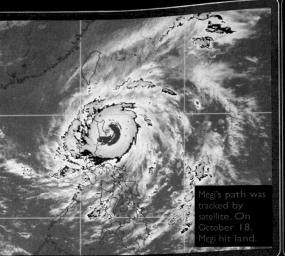

Megi's path was tracked by satellite. On October 18, Megi hit land.

Typhoon Washi, 2011

In December 2011, it was Washi's turn to blast the Philippines, dumping 8 in (20 cm) of rain in just a few hours and causing flash floods more than 3 ft (one meter) deep. Most of the 1,270-plus deaths were due to flooding, which swept away roads, power lines, bridges, and tunnels, and triggered landslides in hilly built-up areas.

Washi's flash floods tossed vehicles around, often into houses.

Typhoon Megi, 2011

Super-typhoons have wind speeds of more than 150 mph (240 km/h). In October 2010, Megi was the only super-typhoon of the Pacific season, with one blast measured at 185 mph (295 km/h). It made landfall on Luzon, Philippines, then pushed on to Taiwan and China. Total deaths were more than 70.

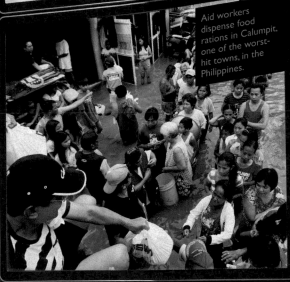

Aid workers dispense food rations in Calumpit, one of the worst-hit towns, in the Philippines.

Philippine police load relief supplies at Cauayan, north Philippines, to airlift south to worst-hit areas.

Typhoon Nesat-Nalgae, 2011

Within a week of each other in late September and early October 2011, typhoons Nesat and Nalgae killed more than 100 people in the Philippines. The first saturated the ground and set off floods; the second worsened an already dire situation. Nesat alone wrecked more than 45,000 houses, and some towns were cut off for more than 10 days.

Haiti QUAKE

On January 12, 2010, the Caribbean nation of Haiti suffered a tremendous 7.0-magnitude earthquake, followed by two strong aftershocks of 5.9 and 5.5 magnitude. The effects were catastrophic—hundreds of thousands were killed and injured and the reconstruction costs are estimated to be $11.5 billion (£7.4 billion).

▼ Haiti's earthquake occured along a strike-slip fault—a break in Earth's crust—where the two sides of the fault slide against each other.

1 Tectonic plates are held in position by the friction between them.

2 Enough pressure builds to overcome this friction, releasing energy as destructive seismic waves.

The origin

The earthquake's center, or focus, was about 8 mi (13 km) underground, 15 mi (24 km) west of the nation's capital, Port-au-Prince. It happened as sections of the Caribbean and North American tectonic plates shifted against each other. The ground shook in some places for up to one minute, and the tremors could be felt as far away as Cuba, 500 mi (800 km) away.

▲ An aerial shot shows the extent of the damage two days after the main earthquake—downtown Port-au-Prince was almost flattened.

The impact

Haiti is a poor nation, with shanty-town buildings and low-standard infrastructure. When the earthquake hit, the effect was disastrous. Many areas were completely flattened. Hospitals, transport, and communications were demolished. People struggled to survive, stranded outside, with little food and great risk of disease.

Rapid relief

A major earthquake destroys infrastructure and leaves people injured, hungry, and homeless. Within a few days international aid workers in Haiti organized essentials such as medicines, food, tents, and fuel.

▲ Haitians clamber aboard a ferry carrying food and medicine to the worst-hit areas of Port-au-Prince.

To the rescue

In several countries around the world, including the U.S., France, Britain, Germany, Japan and Australia, specialist teams of rescue workers are on standby. Within hours of a disaster, they are in action. They bring sophisticated equipment, such as sensors, which detect body heat, faint noises, and even carbon dioxide gas exhaled by people trapped in the rubble.

▶ Rescue workers in Port-au-Prince carefully carry a survivor from a collapsed building.

THE MOST POWERFUL RECORDED QUAKE WAS THE GREAT CHILEAN EARTHQUAKE OF MAY 1960, WITH A MAGNITUDE OF 9.5.

Immense toll

Due to a lack of civilian records, an accurate death toll is unknown. It is thought that 250,000 were killed and 300,000 injured. More than 100,000 homes were lost and thousands of other buildings destroyed. Two million were made homeless, forced to live in temporary shelters.

▼ Huge tent-and-tarpaulin cities were built to house the homeless. Poor sanitation meant that the people were at risk of disease such as cholera.

TWISTER CENTRAL

The world's fastest winds occur in some of its smallest weather features—tornadoes or "twisters." They can materialize almost anywhere, from northern Europe to south Africa, blowing at speeds of more than 125 mph (200 km/h). Some of the fiercest tornadoes ransack the U.S.'s Tornado Alley.

JET STREAM

COLD DRY AIR

WARM DRY AIR

TORNADO ALLEY

South Dakota

Nebraska

Oklahoma

Texas

Along the Alley

Tornado Alley runs from northwest Texas through Oklahoma and Kansas to Nebraska. This is the Great Plains—vast flats, with the Rocky Mountains to the west and Appalachians to the east. Along the Alley, dry, cold air from the Rockies and Canada to the north collides with warm, damp air from the Gulf of Mexico—perfect conditions to form twisters.

Narrow but total

Tornadoes in open farmland damage crops and hit small communities, with a lesser, yet serious, toll. Tracking through built-up areas leaves a long, narrow, intense strip of destruction—as with the twister that hit Joplin, Missouri, in May 2011. Its winds reached 200 mph (320 km/h), and more than 120 people were killed and more than 1,000 injured.

▼ An aerial view of a tornado's straight-line path, in Joplin, 2011.

MORE THAN 80 PERCENT OF TORNADOES OCCUR FROM APRIL·TO JULY, BETWEEN 3 P.M. AND 7 P.M.

Birth of a tornado

Tornadoes form during thunderstorms when warm, moist, light air hits cold, dry, dense air. The cold air forces the warm air up, where its water vapor cools and condenses as rain. Local differences in wind speed make some air masses rotate. Spinning cool air from the base of the thundercloud sinks, stimulating warm air below to whirl and rise. As rotating speeds increase, the swirling mass becomes a narrow column.

Thunderstorm

▶ The column of air that moves upward at the center of a thunderstorm spins, causing it to break through the cloud wall and hit the ground.

Mesocyclone—a powerful air column that moves upward at the center of the storm

Warm air current

Tornado moves across the land in a straight line

Rotating column of air breaks through cloud and hits the ground

Warm front

Cold front

WARM MOIST AIR

THE AVERAGE U.S. TORNADO...

- has a base measuring 500 ft (150 m)
- extends more than 5,000 ft (1,500 m) from the ground to the top
- lasts for around ten minutes
- moves at a speed of 30 mph (50 km/h)
- tears up a track 5 mi (8 km) long
- has wind speeds of at least 65 mph (105 km/h)

▶ A swirling funnel snakes its way through Kansas causing severe damage to buildings.

Inside a twister

The tornado's raging winds whip up surface debris, such as dust, making its lower column visible. Higher up, water vapor condenses into a gray cloudlike funnel. There is often a calmer "eye," like in a hurricane, but the tornado moves so fast, it's difficult to identify.

TOO MUCH WATER

Water is vital for life—but too much drowns life, washes away homes, wrecks buildings and destroys roads. Floods are caused by a number of events—from too much rain and monsoon deluge to glaciers melting and earthquakes breaking riverbanks. In December 2010, Queensland, Australia, felt the full wrath of water's power.

▶ The walls of this house in Ipswich, near Brisbane, were submerged by 10 ft (3 m) of floodwater, leaving just the roof visible.

▼ La Niña occurs across the tropical Pacific Ocean about every five years, bringing extreme weather such as floods and droughts. It causes wetter conditions in Australia, southern Africa, and Southeast Asia, and drier conditions along the coastal regions of Peru, Chile, and southern U.S.

ASIA

NORTH AMERICA

Polar jet stream

Pacific jet stream

AUSTRALASIA

SOUTH AMERICA

A series of causes

Queensland's floods had several probable causes. One was heavy, widespread, persistent rainfall from Cyclone Tasha. This shortlived, forceful storm surged in from the ocean and headed southwest into the state's interior.

Tasha coincided with the La Niña-El Niño cycle—La Niña returns every few years to "oppose" El Niño. It brings cool water temperatures to the ocean's southeast, which then pushes warm, moist, rain-bearing air toward Australia.

Some scientists believe climate change and global warming were also contributing factors. This may only be confirmed in another decade or two.

IN 1931, CHINA'S YELLOW RIVER UNLEASHED A DEVASTATING DELUGE THAT KILLED UP TO FOUR MILLION PEOPLE—THE WORLD'S WORST-EVER NATURAL DISASTER.

Floods damage farmland too This crop of sorghum near Toowoomba, Queensland, was wiped out.

The Big Wet

From December 2010 until January 2011, Australia's northeast state of Queensland suffered mammoth floods. At their worst, the waters affected almost half the state, and the national authorities declared three quarters of Queensland a disaster zone. The torrent flooded coal mines and quarries, washed away roads and rail, and damaged houses and buildings—economic losses are estimated to be more than $11 billion (£7.2 billion).

Flash floods

Queensland's floods got off to a stuttering start in early December with greater-than-usual regular rainfall. Over the Christmas and New Year period, Cyclone Tasha arrived and the rains just kept coming. On January 9–10, 2011, more than 6 in (15 cm) fell in 36 hours on already soaked ground around Toowoomba. Water surged through the city, carrying away cars and trucks and leaving the city center in total ruin.

Brisbane under water

By January 11, 2011, floodwaters flowing east reached the city of Ipswich, near Queensland's capital, Brisbane. The Bremer River here rose nearly 65 ft (20 m). The water bulges continued and in Brisbane itself, its namesake Brisbane River went up 15 ft (4.6 m), swallowing 20,000 homes.

62 mi (100 km) from Brisbane, the town of Grantham was almost destroyed. Police divers had to wade through the floodwaters, searching for survivors.

Greatest ever?

Today's big floods are mere trickles compared to the Zanclean Deluge. Just over five million years ago, massive earth movements opened a narrow channel, now the Strait of Gibraltar, which was then a vast, mostly dried-out basin. Within two years the Mediterranean refilled, sometimes rising 33 ft (10 m) daily, in perhaps the greatest flood the world has ever seen.

STORM OF THE CENTURY

-5°C

EVERY FEW YEARS, A MAJOR STORM ATTACKS!

When certain conditions come together, the result is a "perfect storm" of immense size, power, and ferocity. One such storm occured in eastern North America during March 1993 — the Storm of the Century.

Course of the storm

During early March 1993, low pressure over Mexico moved across the Gulf of Mexico toward Cuba and Florida. It happened to coincide with the jet stream—the high-altitude corridor of rushing air. Cold air was pulled from the far north as the storm tracked northeast over several days, along the Atlantic seaboard into Canada, before fading in late March. This perfect storm became known as the Storm of the Century (SOTC).

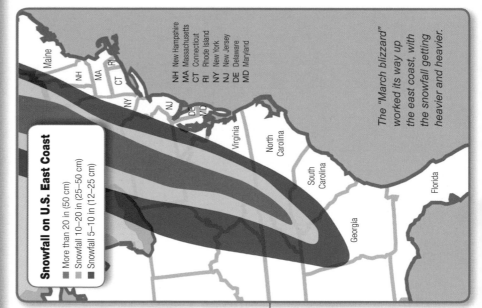

Snowfall on U.S. East Coast

- More than 20 in (50 cm)
- Snowfall 10–20 in (25–50 cm)
- Snowfall 5–10 in (12–25 cm)

Maine

NH
MA
CT RI
NY
NJ
DE
MD

Virginia

North Carolina

South Carolina

Georgia

Florida

NH New Hampshire
MA Massachusetts
CT Connecticut
RI Rhode Island
NY New York
NJ New Jersey
DE Delaware
MD Maryland

The "March blizzard" worked its way up the east coast, with the snowfall getting heavier and heavier.

SOTC STATS

- Other names: Great Blizzard of '93, Superstorm of '93, '93 Nor'easter.
- Date: March 11–16, 1993.
- Maximum snowfall (undrifted): 6 ft (1.8 m).
- Lowest atmospheric pressure: 960 mb.
- Maximum wind gust: Cuba 130 mph (210 km/h), United States 140 mph (225 km/h) on Mount Washington, New Hampshire.
- Boats lost: More than 300 reported but the actual toll was probably three times higher.
- On Long Island alone, 20 homes were lost to the sea due to huge waves.
- More than 150 people were rescued at sea by U.S. Coast Guard in the Gulf of Mexico and Atlantic.
- Electricity outages: Affected a total of more than 100 million people.
- Total volume of water falling as rain, snow, and hail was similar to 40 days of flow of the Mississippi River in New Orleans.

FROM TRAVEL PROBLEMS TO DESTROYED HOMES, THE SOTC AFFECTED MORE THAN ONE THIRD OF THE U.S. POPULATION.

HURRICANE SANDY STATS

- In October 2012 Hurricane Sandy ravaged through the Caribbean and up the east coast of North America.

- At its greatest, Sandy was classed as a category 3 hurricane and measured more than 1,000 mi (1,600 km) across.

- Sandy hit Jamaica, Cuba, and the Bahamas, then moved north off the eastern seaboard to blast ashore in New Jersey.

- In New York City, the storm surge caused power outages and flooding in road tunnels and subways.

- Total damage is estimated at $80 billion (£50 billion), and the death toll close to 300.

HALLOWEEN NOR'EASTER

When conditions really come together, a "perfect storm" of truly exceptional size, power, and ferocity results. The 1991 Halloween Nor'Easter, which spun off Hurricane Grace, inspired the 1997 book and 2000 movie *The Perfect Storm*.

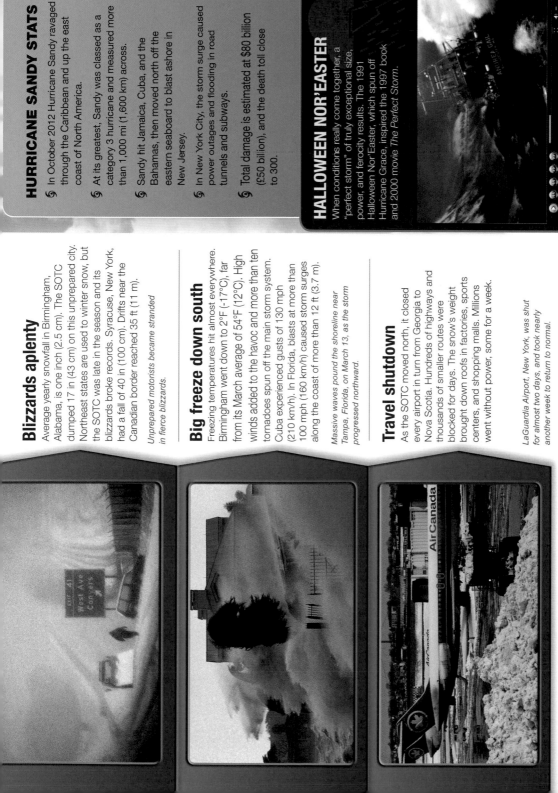

Blizzards aplenty

Average yearly snowfall in Birmingham, Alabama, is one inch (2.5 cm). The SOTC dumped 17 in (43 cm) on this unprepared city. Northeast states are used to winter snow, but the SOTC was late in the season and its blizzards broke records. Syracuse, New York, had a fall of 40 in (100 cm). Drifts near the Canadian border reached 35 ft (11 m).

Unprepared motorists became stranded in fierce blizzards.

Big freeze down south

Freezing temperatures hit almost everywhere. Birmingham went down to 2°F (–17°C), far from its March average of 54°F (12°C). High winds added to the havoc and more than ten tornadoes spun off the main storm system. Cuba experienced gusts of 130 mph (210 km/h). In Florida, blasts at more than 100 mph (160 km/h) caused storm surges along the coast of more than 12 ft (3.7 m).

Massive waves pound the shoreline near Tampa, Florida, on March 13, as the storm progressed northward.

Travel shutdown

As the SOTC moved north, it closed every airport in turn from Georgia to Nova Scotia. Hundreds of highways and thousands of smaller routes were blocked for days. The snow's weight brought down roofs in factories, sports centers, and shopping malls. Millions went without power, some for a week.

LaGuardia Airport, New York, was shut for almost two days, and took nearly another week to return to normal.

INDEX

◄ The limestone cliff face off the shore of the Port Campbell National Park, Australia, has been eroded by the extreme weather conditions from the Southern Ocean.

INDEX

Entries in **bold** refer to main subject entries; entries in *italics* refer to illustrations.

Aborigines 80, 81, 99
abyssal plain 62
acid rain 92, 93
Agulhas Current 53
Al'Aziziya, Libya 40
Alaska, U.S. 65, 73, 74
Aleutian Trench 74
Alpine meadows 103, *103*
Alps **102–3**
Altesch Glacier 103, *103*
aluminum 28, *28*
Amasia 50
Amazon rain forest 21
Amazon River **20–1**
Amundsen, Roald 107
anacondas 88, *88*
Andes Mountains 49
Angel Falls 97, *97*
Antarctic Ocean 51
Antarctica **38–9**, 40
anthropology 87
aragonite crystals 27, *27*
Arches National Park, Utah, U.S. 22
Arctic **38–9**, **50–1**, **106–7**
Arctic foxes 38, *38*
Arctic Ocean 45, 50, 51, 57
Argentino, Lago 24, *24*
Arica, Chile 41
Arizona, U.S. **6–7**
arkose 80, *80*
ash cloud 11, *11*, 15, *15*, 119
ashfalls 139
asteroids 117
Asyût, Egypt 41
Atacama desert, Chile 41
Atlantic Ocean 11, 45, 53, 54, 55, 72, 74
atmosphere 116, 117
atmospheric pressure 57, 148
atolls 60, 61
Augustus, Mount 81, *81*
Aurora Australis (Southern Lights) 9, *9*
Aurora Borealis (Northern Lights) 106, *106*, 107, *107*

aurorae 9, 106, 107
Australia **42–3**, **80–1**, 94, 95, **98–9**, 104, 121, 122, 124, 126, 127, 135, **146–7**
Devil's Marbles 22, *22*
flooding 35, *35*
Austria 138
autonomous underwater vehicles (AUVs) 31
Aval Cliffs, France 76, *76*
avalanches **36–7**, **138–9**
Ayers Rock, Australia **80–1**
Azure Window sea arch 122

Baffin Island 51
Bahamas 44, *44*, 69, 149
Baker, Mount 36
Baltic Sea 73
Bangladesh 134
baobabs 105, *105*
barrier islands 122
barrier reefs **42–3**, 59, **60–1**, **98–9**, 112, *112*
basalt rock 96
Bathurst Bay 121
bats 67, 110
bauxite 28, *28*
Bay of Bengal 76
Bay of Fundy 120
beaches 77
bears 38, *38*, 50, 107, *107*
Bedouins 101
Beichuan County, China 18, *18*
Belize 112
Bengal tigers 76
Bikini Atoll 61
biodiversity 87, 99
bioluminescence 68
birds 81, 83, *83*, 91, 101, 106
black and white smokers 31, *31*, 63, *63*
Black Hole of Andros 69, *69*
Black Sea 76
blind fish 110, 111
blizzards 37, 133, 149
blue jets 35
blue Moon 35
Bolivia 88, **90–1**
Brazil **84–5**, 88, 135

Bryce Canyon 82, *82*
bubble curtains 66
Bunyip State Park, Australia 127
buran 133
Burma 134
Burringurrah 81, *81*
bushfires 41, *41*, 126, 127

cacti 90, *90*
caimans 88, *88*
calcium carbonate 27
calderas 86
Californian condors 83, *83*
Camel Corps 101, *101*
Canada 120
canyons 22, *22*, 44, 62, **82–3**, 96, 100, 101
Cape Horn 55
Cape of Good Hope 52
Cappadocia 94
capybaras 89, *89*
carbon dioxide 46, 70
Caribbean Sea 72
catsharks 70
cattle ranching 89
cave lions 25, *25*
caverns 136, 137
caves **26–7**, 38, *38*, 93, *93*, 110, 111
cell phones 28, *28*
cenotes **110–11**
Chaiten volcano 131
chalk 95
Challenger Deep 74
Chamonix, France 37
Chicxulub, Mexico 8
Chile 127, 131, 143, 146
China 92, 120, 125, 135, 136, 139, 141, 147
chital deer 76, *76*
Christ the Redeemer statue 85, *85*
cinder cones 109
cliffs 76, 77
climate change 51, 53, 63, 123, 146
clouds 34, *34*, 56, 57, 130, *130*
coal 28, *28*, 71
coastal erosion 23, *23*, **122–3**
coastlines **76–7**, **122–3**

Colorado River 23, *23*, 82, *82*, 83
coltan 28, *28*
Columbia 139
columns and pillars **94–5**
comets 9
Concepcion, Chile 18
condors 83, *83*
Congo 135
Congo River 20
continental plates 49, 63, 73
continental shelf 67, *67*
Copacabana Beach 84, *84*
copper 29, *29*
coral reefs **42–3**, 59, **60–1**, **98–9**,
    112, *112*
Corcovado 85
core, Earth's 10, *10*
Coriolis Force 57
Cotton Castle (Pamukkale) 17, *17*
cowboys 89, *89*
crabs 62, *62*, 70
craters 15, *15*, 118
crocodilians 88, *88*, 112
crocuses 101, *101*
Cuba 148, 149
cumulonimbus clouds 56, 130, *130*
currents, ocean **52–3**, 121
cyclones **32–3**, 57, 72, 121, 123,
    140–1, 146, 149

Daisetta sinkhole, Texas, U.S. 137,
    137
Dakhla Oasis, Egypt 41
dams 140
Danube Delta 76, *76*
Darwin, Charles 61
Dead Sea 47, 113, *113*
Death Valley, U.S. 40, *40*
deep-sea exploration **30–1**
deep-sea zone **62–3**, **30–1**
DeepSee submersible 30, *30*
Deepwater Horizon oil rig 29, *29*
deer 76, *76*
deforestation 87, 112
deltas 76, *76*
Democratic Republic of the Congo 14,
    112
derecho 132
desert larks 101, *101*

desertification 125
deserts **40–1**, 124
destruction, habitats **112–13**
Devil's Marbles, Australia 22, *22*
Devil's Pool 97, *97*
diamonds 29, *29*
dinosaurs 111
diving 38, *38*
dolomite 136
dolphins 21, *21*, 66
downburst winds 132, 133
droughts 125, 146
dumbo octopus 30, *30*, 62, *62*
Dungeness Spit 77, *77*
Dunwich 122
dust storms **124–5**, 133

Earth's crust **10–11**, **48–9**, 58, 123,
    128
  formation **116–17**
  mantle 123
earthquakes **18–19**, 49, 65, 73, 74,
    128, 129, **142–3**
East Africa 126
East African Rift System 86, *87*
East Pacific Rise 48, *48*
Easter Island 75
echolocation 66, 67
ecosystems 60, 70, 76, 86, 89, 99,
    113
El Niño 146
energy
  renewable 71
  solar 56
  thermal 52
England 120, 122, 135
erosion **6–7**, **22–3**, 80, 81, 82, 85,
    93, 94, 95, 96, 101, 103, **122–3**,
    138
estuaries 120
Everest, Mount **12–13**, 74
Everglades 113, *113*
evolution 87, 105
Exxon Valdez disaster 75
Eyjafjallajökull volcano, Iceland 11

fairy chimneys 94, *94*
Faisal Bin Hussein, Prince 100
fault lines 86

faults (Earth's crust) 18
feldspars 80
Ferdinandea 59, *59*
Fiji 71
firebreaks 126
fire, wild 41, *41*, **126–7**
fishing 70, 71, 74, 99
fjords 51, 106
flamingos 91
floods 35, *35*, 51, 88, 89, *89*, 90,
    121, 128, 135, 140, 141, **146–7**
Florida, U.S. 113, 136, 137, 149
fluorite 28, *28*
formation, Earth's **116–17**
fossils 91, 136
foxes 38, 101
France 103
frogs 105
Fujita scale 145
Fukushima Nuclear Power Plant,
    Japan 129

Galapagos Islands 75
Galveston, U.S. 33
geysers **16–17**, 31, *31*
Ghudamis, Libya 40
giant ostracod 31, *31*
glaciation 103
glaciers **24–5**, 51, *51*, 103, *103*, 106,
    119, 139
Global Conveyor **52–3**
global warming 51, 53, 87, 92, 99,
    123, 146
Godzilla (chimney) 63
gold 46
gold leaf 29, *29*
Gondwana 104, *104*
Gondwanaland 49
Goreme National Park, Turkey 94, *94*
gorillas, mountain 112, 113
Grace, Hurricane 149
Grand Canyon, Arizona, U.S. 23, *23*,
    82–3
granite 95, 104
graphite 28, *28*
gravity 54, 116, 117
Great Bahama Canyon 44
Great Barrier Reef **42–3**, 61, **98–9**
Great Dune of Pyla 77

Great Plains, U.S. 144
Great Rift Valley **86–7**, 100
green sea turtles 70, *70*
Greenland 39
Guatemala 137
Gulf of California 75
Gulf of Mexico 72, 148
Gulf of Tonkin 92
Gunung Mulu caves, Borneo 27, *27*
guyots 59
gypsum 29, *29*
gyres 52

habitat loss 83, 112, 113
haboob 41, *41*, 124
hail 56
hailstones 34, 130, 131
Haiti **142–3**
Halloween Nor'Easter 149
Halong Bay **92–3**
Hawaii 15, 48, 55, **108–9**
hematite 28, *28*
Himalayas **12–13**
hoodoos 22, *22*, 82, *82*
hot springs 17
hotspots 58
Hubbard glacier 25, *24–5*
human ancestors 87
Hunga Ha'apai 59, *59*
hunting 89
Hurricane Katrina 33, *33*
hurricanes **32–3**, 57, 72, 121, 123,
    140–1, 146, 149
hydrogen 47
hydrothermal vents 31, 63

ibex 101
ice ages 25, 51
ice islands 50
ice sheets 39, *39*
icebergs 25, 39, 50, 51, **106**, *106*
Iceland 11, *11*
igneous rocks 80, *80*
India 134, 135
Indian Ocean 61, 74
  mega-tsunami 19, *19*
international aid 143
International Ice Patrol 51
iron oxides 80

islands 123
  coral 60, 61
  creation of **58–9**
Italy 102

jaguar 88
Jamaica 149
Japan **128–9**, 138
Jason ROV (remotely operated
    vehicle) 31
jellyfish 68, *68*, 99, *99*
jet stream 148
jewels 29, *29*
Jordan **100–1**, 113

K-P event 8
karst landscapes 26, 92, 93
Kata Tjuta 81, *81*
Katmai, Mount 74
Kebili, Tunisia 40
kelp 65, 75
Kenya 125
Ketsana, Typhoon 140
Kilauea 109, *109*
Kilimanjaro, Mount 25, 87, *87*
Komodo National Marine Park 45, 75
Kongsfjorden 106
Kongsvegen 106, *106*

La Niña 146
lagoons 60
lahars 119, 139
Lake Malawi 87, *87*
Lake Minchin 90
Lake Tanganyika 87
Lake Victoria 87
landslides **138–9**, 140, 141
Las Vegas, U.S. 40, *40*
Late Heavy Bombardment 117
lava 14, *14*, 48, 58, 59, 108, *108*,
    109, *109*, 116, 119
Law of the Sea Treaty 45
Lawrence, T.E. (Lawrence of Arabia)
    100
lemurs 105, *105*
life, earliest 117
light, underwater **68–9**
lightning 35, *35*, 83, **114–15**, 126,
    131

limestone 26, 92, 93, 94, 95, 105,
    111, 122, 136, 137
lions 25, *25*
lithium 90
Little Salt Spring sinkholes 136
living fossils 99
lobsters 63, *63*
loggerhead turtles 54, *54*
Loltun Caves 111
Lot's Wife 95
Louisiana 122

Maasai people 86, *86*
macaque monkeys 17, *17*
mackerel 70
macroburst winds 133
Madagascar **104–5**
maelstroms 64, 121
magma 15, *15*, 48, 58, 118
Mahina, Tropical Cyclone 121
Maldives 60, 61
Malta 122
mammatus clouds 34, *34*
Mammoth Cave, Kentucky, U.S. 27
manatees 112
mangrove swamps 76, *76*
manta rays 45
mantle, Earth's 86, *86*, 109
marble 28, *28*
Mariana Trench 30, 63, *63*, 74
marine snow 30
marine wildlife sanctuaries 75
Martinique 73, 139
Matobo Hills 95, *95*
Matterhorn 102, *102*
Mauna Kea 64, 109, *109*
Mauna Loa 108, *108*
Mayans 111
Mediterranean Sea 59
mega-tsunamis 19, *19*
Megi, Typhoon 141
Mekong River 34, *34*
mercury 28, *28*
metals 29
metamorphic rocks 80, *80*
meteorites 111, 117
meteors 8, *8*
Mexico **110–11**
microbes 117

microburst winds 132, 133
Mid-Atlantic Ridge 11
mid-ocean ridges 48, *48*, 58, 63
midnight sun 39, *39*
minerals **28–9**, 46, 61, 63
mining 66, 67
Mohave Desert, U.S. 40
Mongolia 133
monkeys 17, *17*
monoliths **80–1**, **100–1**
monsoons 134–5
Mont Blanc 103
Monterey Bay 75
Montserrat 139
Moon 120
Moon, blue 35
moraines 103
mountain gorillas 112, 113
mountaineering 102, 104, *104*
mountains **12–13**, 14, 16, 25, 36,
    37, 48, 49, 64, 74, 81, *81*, 87,
    102–3
  Andes Mountains 49
  Mount Augustus 81, *81*
  Mount Baker 36
  Mount Everest **12–13**, 74
  Mount Katmai 74
  Mount Kilimanjaro 25, 87, *87*
  Mount Olga 81
  Mount Pelée 73, 139
  Sugarloaf Mountain 85, *85*
movie locations 100, *100*, 101
mudslides 119, 138, 139
mythology 93, 108

Nagano, Japan 17
Nalgae, Typhoon 141
natural disasters 72–3
  earthquakes **18–19**, 49, 65, 73, 74,
    128, 129, **142–3**
  floods 35, *35*, 51, 88, 89, *89*, 90,
    121, 128, 135, 140, 141, **146–7**
  tsunamis 19, *19*, 73, **128–9**
  volcanoes 10, *10*, 11, **14–15**,
    14–15, 16, 35, 48, 49, 58–9, *59*,
    60, 61, 63, 73, 74, 85, 86, *86*,
    87, 91, **108–9**, *108–9*, 116, 117,
    118–19, 123, 131, 139
natural gas 71, 75

nautiluses 99, *99*
Nebraska, U.S. 32, *32*
Needles, The, U.K. *95*
nephology 34
Nesat, Typhoon 141
Netherlands 121
Nevado del Ruiz volcano 139
Ngorongoro Crater 86, *86*
nickel 29, *29*
Nile River 20
nomadic pastoralism 86, 101
North Africa 125
North Pole 51, 57
Northern Lights 106, *106*, 107, *107*
nutrients 46, 51, 53
Nyiragongo volcano 14

ocean depth 44, 74
ocean floor 58, 62, 63
ocean trenches 49, 63, 74
oceanic plates 48, 49, 58, 63, 73
oceans 11, **30–1**, 39, **44–77**, **120–1**
  currents **52–3**, 121
  deep ocean **30–1**, **62–3**
  formation of 45
  Pacific Ocean 55, **74–5**
  records **64–5**
  waves **54–5**
octopuses 30, 62, *62*, 68
oil 29, *29*, 71, *71*, 75
Old Faithful geyser 16, *16*
Olduvai Gorge 86, 87
Olga, Mount 81
Olgas **81**
oppossum shrimps 69, *69*
ostracod, giant 31, *31*
outgassings 118
oxygen 46, 47, 69
oysters 71, *71*

Pacific Ocean 27, *31*, 55, **74–5**
Pacific Plate 74
Pacific Ring of Fire 10
Painted Cliffs, Tasmania 23, *23*
Pakistan 134, 135
Pamukkale (Cotton Castle) 17, *17*
Pangaea 49
Pantanal **88–9**
Panthalassa 49

Paraguay 88
Parana River 20
parasitic craters 118
Paria Wilderness Area, Arizona, U.S.
    7, *7*
pearl farms 71
Pelée, Mount 73, 139
penguins 25, *25*, 38, *38*
"perfect storm" 148, 149
Perito Morengo glacier 24, *24*
Persian Gulf 57
Peru 146
Philippines **140–1**
Phoenix, Arizona 124
photosynthesis 77, 98
phytoplankton 73
Piccard, Jacques 30
pinnacles 82, *82*, **94–5**
Pinnacles Desert, Australia 95, *95*
planets 116
plankton 53, 69
plants 81, 88, 90, 101, 103, *103*, 105
plastic waste 70, 71
plate tectonics **10–11**, 18, **48–9**,
    73, 74, 86, *86*, 101, 103, 109,
    123, 128, 142
polar bears 38, *38*, 50, 107, *107*
pollution **70–1**, 73, 75, 89, 99, 112
Polynesian Islands 75
polyps 98, *98*, 99
Port Campbell National Park, Australia
    122
prairies 126
prawns 70
protoplanets 116, 117
pteropods 62, *62*
pyroclastic flows 119, 139

Qiantang River 120
Qingquan sinkhole 136, *136*
Queensland, Australia *35*, **146–7**

radio waves 66
rain, acid 92, 93
rain forest 21, 105
rainbows 107
rainfall 56, 57
  average 135
  monsoons **134–5**

Red Sea 64, 86
red sprites 35
remotely operated vehicles (ROVs) 31
reptiles 81, 88, 101, 110, **112**
Rhodes, Cecil 95
Richter scale 118
Ring of Fire 74
Rio de Janeiro **84–5**
rivers
  Amazon River **20–1**
  Colorado River 23, *23*, 82, *82*, 83
  Congo River 20
  Mekong River 34, *34*
  Nile River 20
  Parana River 20
  Qiantang River 120
  Urubamba River 20
  Yangtze River 20
  Yellow River 147
  Yenisei River 20
  Zambezi River 96, 97
rock art 80, *80*
rock pools 77
rock stacks 94, *94*
rockfalls 139
ROVs (remotely operated vehicles) 31
Rubbataha Reefs 75

sacred sites 80, 81, 111
Sahara desert 41, *41*, 124
Sahel 125
Salar de Uyuni **90–1**
salt domes 137
salt extraction 90, *90*, 113
salt flats **90–1**
Saltstraumen 64
salty water 46, 47, 64
San Francisco earthquake 19, *19*
sand dunes 41, 77
sand-blasting 22
sandstone 7, *7*, 80, 100, 101, 136
sandstorms **124–5**
Sandy, Hurricane 149
Sarawak, Borneo 27, *27*
Sargasso Sea 54
satellite images 44, *44*, 47, *47*
Saudi Arabia 125, 135
savanna 126
Scandinavia 51

Scheveningen 121
Scilly Isles, U.K. 53
scorpionfish 59
scree 139
sea arches 77, *77*, 122, *122*
sea ice 46, 50, 51, 53, 57
sea levels 92
  changes 44, 50, 51, 54, 61
  rising 123
sea otters 75
sea stacks 77
seamounts 59
sedimentary rocks 80, *80*, 83, 100
seismic waves 18, 142
seismometers 118, 119
Sentry (AUV) 31
Severn Bore 120, *120*
shield volcanoes 109
shockwaves 116, 131
shooting stars (meteor showers) 8, 9
shrimps 68, 69, *69*
sinkholes 26, *26*, 69, *69*, 93,
  136–7
slash-and-burn cultivation 89, 112
slider turtles 110, *110*
slot canyons 22, *22*
snakes 88, *88*, 101
snowfall 24, **36–7**, 130, 133, 148,
  149
  avalanches 138–9
  blizzards 133, 149
  snowbows 107, *107*
  snowflakes 36, *36*
SOFAR (SOund Fixing and Ranging)
  Channel 67
solar energy 56
Solar System 116
solar winds 107
sonar 67
Soufrière Hills volcano 139
sounds
  speed of sound 66
  underwater **66–7**
South China Basin 75
South Pole 51, 57
Southern Lights 9
Southern Ocean 45, 51
space debris 117
spectacled caimans 88, *88*

spelunkers 27, *27*
sperm whales 64
spiders 105
spiny sea horse 77, *77*
Spirit Lake 119
spits 77
Spitsbergen 106
sponges 71
squall lines 132
St. Helens, Mount, U.S. 14, 16,
  118–19
St. Lucia 123
stalactites 111, 26, *26*
stalagmites 26, *26*, 93
steel 28, *28*
storm chasers 33, *33*
storm drains 135
storm surges 121, 149
storms **32–3**, 52, 57, **72–3**,
  114–15, 117, 121, 122, **130–3**
  dust storms **124–5**, 133
  sandstorms **124–5**
  Storm of the Century (SOTC) **148–9**
  thunderstorms 121, 124, **130–1**,
    132, 145
  volcanic electrical storms 131
Strait of Gibraltar 147
stromatolites 46, *46*
subduction zones 74
submarines 30, 31
submersibles 63, *63*, 30, *30*
Sudan 41, *41*
Sugarloaf Mountain 85, *85*
sulfur dioxide 118
Sun 116, 120
  halos 34, *34*
Sunderbans 76
sundogs 34, *34*
sunfish 46, *46*
sunrises and sunsets 81, *81*, 82
super-typhoons 141
supercell storms 32, *32*, 130
supercontinents 104
supernovae 116
supervolcanoes 16
surfing 55, *55*
Surtsey 123
Svalbard **106–7**
swallowholes 136

sweetlips fish 99, *99*
Switzerland 102

Taiwan 55, 141
Talas, Tropical Storm 138
Tanzania 86
Tasha, Cyclone 146
Taupo, Lake 15
tectonic plates **10–11**, 18, **48–9**,
  73, 74, 86, *86*, 101, 103, 109,
  123, 128, 142
temperatures 47, 57, 58, 63
  coldest 39
  hottest 40
thalassophobia 76
Thelma, Typhoon 140
thermal currents 83
thermal energy 52
thermoregulation 57
Thor's Hammer 82
thunderstorms 121, 124, **130–1**,
  132, 145
tidal bores 120, *120*
tides **54–5**, 64, 77, **120–1**
timber industry 113
Tip, Typhoon 140
Titanic 25, 51
Tomas, Hurricane 123
Tornado Alley, Great Plains, U.S. 33,
  144–5
tornadoes 32, *32*, 34, 133, **144–5**,
  149
Torres Strait Islanders 99
tourism 82, 84, 85, 90, 97, 99
Trieste submersible 30
tropical cyclones **32–3**, 57, 72, 121,
  123, **140–1**, 146, 149
Tsaranoro Massif 104, *104*
tsingy 105, *105*
tsunamis 19, *19*, 73, **128–9**
tubeworms 63, *63*
Turkey 94
turtles 54, *54*, 70, *70*, 110, *110*, 112
Twelve Apostles, Australia 94, *94*
typhoons **32–3**, 57, 72, 121, 123,
  140–1, 146, 149

Uluru, Australia **80–1**
undercutting 123

underground rivers 136
UNESCO World Heritage Sites 76
Ungava Bay 120
universe, creation **8–9**
updrafts 131
Urubamba River 20
USA **6–7**, **82–3**, **118–19**, 122, 124,
  126, 130, 135, 136, 137, **144–5**,
  148–9

Venezuela 97, 138
Vesuvius, Mount 15
Victoria Falls 96, *96*, **78–9**
Vietnam **92–3**
Virunga National Park 112, *112*
volcanoes 10, *10*, 11, **14–15**, 16,
  35, 48, 49, 59, *59*, 60, 61, 63,
  73, 74, 85, 86, *86*, 87, 91,
  108–9, 116, 117, **118–19**, 123,
  131, 139
volcanologists 109
Vostock, Antarctica 39
Vredefort, South Africa 9

Wadi Rum **100–1**
Waimangu geyser, New Zealand 16
Walsh, Don 30
Washi, Typhoon 141
water
  color 68, 69
  composition of **46–7**
  seawater, total volume of 44
  vapor 45, 47, 56, 121, 130, 131
water cycle 56, *56*
waterfalls **78–9**, **96–7**
waterspouts 34, *34*, 121, *121*
waves 23, *23*, **54–5**, 65, 77
weather 21, *21*, **32–3**, **34–5**, 52,
  56–7
weathering **6–7**, **22–3**, 80, 81, 82,
  85, 93, 94, 95, 96, 101, 103,
  122–3, 138
wetlands 76, **88–9**, *88–9*
whirlpools 64, 121, *121*
White Nile 87
white pelicans 76
wildfires 41, *41*, **126–7**
wildlife 81, 83, 88, 89, 91, 98, 99,
  101, 105, 107, 110, 111, 112

winds **32–3**, 55, 57, 76, 124, 130,
  132–3, **144–5**, 148
  buran 133
  cyclones/hurricanes/typhoons
    32–3, 57, 72, 121, 123, **140–1**,
    146, 149
  derecho 132
  downbursts 132, 133
  macrobursts 133
  microbursts 132, 133
  tornadoes 32, *32*, 34, 133, **144–5**,
    149
woolly mammoth 25, *25*

Xiaozhai Tiankeng sinkhole 136

Yangtze River 20
Yellow River 147
Yellowstone Park, U.S. 16
Yenisei River 20
yeti crabs 62, *62*
Yonge Reef 98, *98*
Yucatán Peninsula **110–11**

Zambezi River 96, 97
Zambia 96
Zanclean Deluge 147
Zimbabwe 95, 96
zones, deep-sea 31
zooxanthellae algae 98

ACKNOWLEDGMENTS

The publishers would like to thank the following sources for the use of their photographs:

KEY

A/AL=Alamy, B=Bridgeman, CO=Corbis, D=Dreamstime, F=Fotolia, FLPA=Frank Lane Picture Agency, GI=Getty Images, GW=Glow Images, IS=istockphoto.com, MP=Minden Pictures, N=Newscom, NG=National Geographic Creative, NPL=Nature Picture Library, P=Photoshot, PL=Photolibrary, R=Reuters, RF=Rex Features, S=Shutterstock, SJC=Stuart Jackson-Carter, SPL=Science Photo Library, SS=Superstock, TF=Topfoto

t=top, a=above, b=bottom/below, c=center, l=left, r=right, f=far, m=main, bg=background

FRONT COVER Nasa/Npeter/S, SPINE Smileus/S, BACK COVER Minerva Studio/S, muratart/S, Robynrg/S, Volodymyr Goinyk/S, PRELIMS 1 grandboat/S, 2–3 4 S, andrej pol/S, 5 Francesco R. Iacomino/S, Pierpaolo Romano/S

ACTIVE EARTH 6–7 Adam Jones/SPL 8–9(m) NASA Earth Observatory/SPL, (l) Tony Craddock/SPL, (tr) NASA-JSC-ES&IA, (frame) Shawn Hine/S, (br) Gordon Garradd/SPL 10–11(bg) Jose AS Reyes/S, (m) mangiurea 10(l) Andrea Danti, (br) George Steinmetz/CO 11(tl) Vitaly Korovin, (tr) Michael Peuckert/P, (br) Arctic-Images/Corbis 12–13(m) Grant Dixon/MP/FLPA 12(c) Doug Allan/NPL, (frame) imagestock/iS, 13(cr) Galen Rowell/Corbis, (br) Valentyn Volkov/S 14–15(c) Vulkanette/S, (cb) Doug Perrine 14(bl) Peter Oxford/NPL/RF 15(tr) Alexander Gatsenko/S 16 Carlyn Iverson/SPL 17(t) Michael Krabs/ Imagebroker/FLPA, (cr) Nadezda/S, (b) Dr. Richard Roscoe, Visuals Unlimited/SPL 18–19(bg) KPA/Zuma/RF 18(cl) Gary Hinks/SPL, (br) Sipa Press/RF 19(tr) UC Regents, Natl. Information Service For Earthquake Engineering/SPL, (cl) Corbis, (br) dpa/Corbis 20–1(water bg) Dudarev Mikhail/S, (bl) Aaron Amat/S, (tl) Frank Siteman/Science Faction, (cl) Jacques Jangoux/Peter Arnold Images/P, (cr) Kevin Schafer/MP/FLPA, (tr) Kevin Schafer/MP/ FLPA, (br) Planetobserver/SPL 22(bg) Jack Dykinga/NPL, (c) Scott Prokop/S, (b) Konstantin Sutyagin/GI 23(bg) ImageState, (sign tr) Steve Collender/S and dusan964/S, (m) Albo/F, (sign b) Lou Oates/S, (b) Grant Dixon/MP/FLPA 24–5(m) Bernhard Edmaier/ SPL, (bl) Marcos Brindicci/Reuters/Corbis, (paper tr) pdtnc/F, (br) Colin Monteath/P 26–7(m) Steven Kazlowski/Science Faction/Corbis 26(c) KeystoneUSA-ZUMA/RF, (paper cl) Alexey Khromushin/F, (sign br) marekuliasz/S 27(sign tl) Steve Collender/S, (sign tr) maxkovalev/S, (cl) Ashley Cooper/Corbis, (cr) Carsten Peter/Speleoresearch & Films/GI, (sign bl) Lou Oates/S, (br) Tony Waltham/RHWI/Corbis 28–9(bg) Mirek Hejnicki/S, sspopov/S, SeDmi/S, kilukilu/S and leolintang/S; (objects on conveyor belt, l–r, t–b) Serhiy Shullye/S, Outsider/S, E.R.Degginger/S, Picsfive/S, Denis Selivanov/S, Keith Wilson/S, Konovalikov Andrey/S, Alexander Kalina/S, Bragin Alexey/S, Jean-Claude Revy, ISM/SPL, Kamil Krzaczynski/epa/Corbis, Juri/S,

dslaven/S, Krasowit/S, Jens Mayer/S, stocksnapp/S, Maria Brzostowska/F, Steve Vidler/P, Jason Reed/Reuters/Corbis; (tr) Jon T. Fritz/MCT 30(tr frame) diak/S, (tr) NPL, (gold plate) Alaettin YildIrim/S, (cr) Argus/S, (bl) Jeffrey L. Rotman 31(tr) Victor Habbick Visions/SPL, (cl) NPL/RF, (laptop bl) Edhar/S, (bl) Dr Ken Macdonald/SPL, (br) Jamie Cross/S 32–3(bg) Planetobserver/SPL 32(t–b, l–r) John Wollworth/S, Mike Hollingshead/Science Faction/Corbis, Jim Reed/Jim Reed Photography – Severe &/Corbis, dswebb/iS 33(t–b, l–r) Caitlin Mirra/S, jam4travel/S, Carsten Peter/GI, Irwin Thompson/Dallas Morning News/Corbis 34(m) Gene Rhoden/P, (c)Gallo Images/GI, (bl) AFP/GI, (br) Jim Reed/FLPA 35(tl) Olivier Vandeginste/SPL, (tr) mtkang/S, (c) Ivan Cholakov Gostock-dot-net/S, (b) AFP/GI 36–7(m) Scott Warren/P 36(bl) Joel Blit/S, (br) Steve Collender/S 37(bl) Picimpact/Corbis, (c) Brandelet/S 38–9(tm) Ward Kennan/P, (t, l–r) Dan Burton/NPL, AlaskaStock/P, Planetary Visions Ltd/SPL, (bm) Juniors Bildarchiv/P, (b, l–r) George Steinmetz/Corbis, Frans Lanting/Corbis, Planetary Visions Ltd/SPL 40(bg) Sasha Buzko, (tl) Tischenko Irina/S, (cl) Anan Kaewkhammul/S, (cr) Mikhail/S, (frame, bl) imagestock, (bl) Kordcom Kordcom/P 41(tl) Michael Freeman/Corbis, (frame c) Cre8tive Images/S, (c) T Carrafa/Newspix/RF, (r) Anan Kaewkhammul/S

VAST OCEANS 42–3 Ingo Arndt/NPL, 44–5(bg) r.classen/S, 44(br) NASA/SPL, 44(cl) NASA/SPL, 45(br) Mathieu Meur/ Stocktrek Images/CO, 45(tr) Lynette Cook/SPL, 46–7(beaker) janprchal/S, 46–7(bg) Henrik Winther Andersen/S, 46(bc) nito/S, 46(br) Doug Perrine/GI, 46(cl) Iraidka/S, 46(cr) Franco Banfi/GI, 46(l) photovova/S, 46(l) Alliance/S, 47(br) DenisNata/S, 47(tr) NASA/SPL, 48–9 SJC, 48–9(bg) Alexandr79/S, 48(bl) Doug Perrine/NPL, 48(cr) Dr Ken Macdonald/SPL, 49(cr) Imagebroker, Johannes Pfatschbach/Imagebroker/FLPA, 49(tr) SJC, 48–9(bg) Sergey Nivens/S, 50(r) Ole Jorgen Liodden/NPL, 51(br) NASA/Goddard Space Flight Center Scientific Visualization Studio, 51(l) Biosphoto/SuperStockBiosphoto/SS, 52–3(bg on cards) Magnia/S, 52–3(bg) severija/S, 52–3(c) Pyty/S, 52–3(game pieces) Timof/S, 52(l) Mariusz Kluzniak/GI, 52(tl bg) Adrian Hillman/Fotolia, 53(tc) P, 53(tr) Mariel Stenzel/NG, 54–5(bg) EpicStockMedia/S, 54–5(bg) MJTH/S, 54–5(tattoo) TSHIRT-FACTORYdotCOM/S, 54(bc) Brian J. Skerry/NG, 54(bl) bigro/S, 54(br) Nanna Studio/S, 54(c) Gary Hincks/SPL, 54(cl) grafiz/S, 55(c) Design Pics Inc/RF, 55(c) S, 55(t) Flip De Nooyer/ Foto Natura/Minden Pictures/CO, 56–7(c) Patrickma/S, 57(b) vectorOK/S, 57(bc) joinanita/S, 57(br) cartoons/S, 57(c) Zern Liew/S, 58–9(bg) DVARG/S, 58–9(bg) andersphoto/S, 58–9 AFP/GI, 58(br) Lothar Slabon/epa/CO, 58(tl, bl) Crepesoles/S, 59(b) Volga/S, 59(br) Eurelios/SPL, 59(tl, br) Borislav Bajkic/S, 59(tr) Franco Banfi/Biosphoto/FLPA, 60–1(bg) s oleg/S, 60(bc) grintan/S, 60(bg bl) inxti/S, 60(bg tl) LiliGraphie/S, 60(br) S, 60(cr) Franco Banfi/NPL, 60(tr) My Good Images/S, 61(b, cr) BrAt82/S, 61(bc) Colin Marshall/FLPA, 61(bg tr) Leigh Prather/S, 61(bl) Michael Friedel/

121(b) DICK TESKE/EPA, 121(c) PS, 121(cr) M_G/S,
122–3 Philippe Hays/RF, 122(br) trekandshoot/S, 122(tc) Visuals
Unlimited/CO, 122(tc) Raia/S, 122(tr) MarcelClemens/S,
123(br) Yves Regaldi/ZenShui/CO, 123(tc) Ashley Cooper/
SpecialistStock/SplashdownDirect/RF, 123(tc) Joe Gough/S,
124–5 Daniel J Bryant/GI, 124(br) NASA/SPL, 124(tl) Tim
Wimborne/R, 124(tl) FotoSergio/S, 125(br) Imaginechina/CO,
125(tr) Tim Wimborne/R, 125(tr) MaraZe/S, 126–7 Petrosg/S,
126(l) James Warwick/GI, 126(r) KARI GREER/SPL, 126(tl) Sergey
Mironov/S, 126(tl) Hefr/S, 127(l) Frans Lanting/CO, 127(r) Lucas
Dawson/GI, 127(t) Vividz Foto/S, 127(tl) AFP/GI,
128–9 KeystoneUSA-ZUMA/RF, 128–9(b) Aflo/RF, 128(bl) JOSE
ANTONIO PEÑAS/SPL, 128(cr) S, 129(bc) KeystoneUSA-ZUMA/RF,
129(cr) Pakhnyushcha/S, 130–1 G.J. McCarthy/AP/PA,
130–1 WOLF AVNI/S, 130–1(bg) S, 130(bl) S, 130(bl) NASA/SPL,
130(t) ARENA Creative/S, 130(tr) Chad Cowan/RF,
130(tr) nuttakit/S, 131(br) mmm/S, 131(c) R, 131(c) Piyato/S,
132–3 PEKKA PARVIAINEN/SPL, 132–3(bg) StudioSmart/S,
132(bl) NASA/CO, 132(bl) Linali/S, 132(br) Chubykin Arkady/S,
132(t) fluidworkshop/S, 133(br) Hamid Sardar/CO, 134–5 AFP/GI,
134(bl) Jagdish Agarwal/CO, 134(br) 1000 Words/S, 134(l) Neale
Cousland/S, 134(tl) jesadaphorn/S, 135(b) AFP/GI,
135(br) marekuliasz/S, 135(br) fotosutra.com/S, 135(br) Diana
Taliun/S, 135(cl) Igor Kovalchuk/S, 135(tc) cristovao/S,
136–7 DANIEL LECLAIR/X002/Reuters/CO, 136(bl) Liveshot/S,
136(bl) James Nielsen/AP/PA, 137(bl) Roxana Gonzalez/S,
137(br) Stringer Shanghai/R, 137(t) ZUMA/RF, 138–9 mdd/S,
138–9 Michael Woessner/S, 138–9(bg) Scott Prokop/S,
138(br) JACK HAIJES/EPA, 138(cl) SergeyDV/S, 138(cl) JJ
Studio/S, 138(cr) Lev Kropotov/S, 138(tl) Styve Reineck/S,
138(tr) KeystoneUSA-ZUMA/RF, 138(tr) the808/S, 139(br) PABLO
SANCHEZ/CO, 139(br) Andrzej Gibasiewicz/S, 139(br) ermess/S,
139(cl) Sipa Press/RF, 139(cl) Tim Burrett/S, 139(tl) Greg
Epperson/S, 139(tr) Stocktrek Images/SS , 140–1 Vladislav
Gurfinkel/S, 140–1 Sundari/S, 140–1(b) PozitivStudija/S,
140–1(bc) Jose Gil/S, 140–1(bg) Daboost/S, 140(bc) Fenton
one/S, 140(bc) Denys Prykhodov/S, 140(br) DENNIS M.
SABANGAN/epa/CO, 140(tr) AFP/GI, 141(bc) Asianet-Pakistan/S,
141(bc) KAMONRAT/S, 141(bl) AFP/GI, 141(cr) ROLEX DELA PENA/
epa/CO, 141(tl) Rouelle Umali/Xinhua Press/CO, 141(tr)
KeystoneUSA-ZUMA/RF, 142–3 Thirteen/S, 142–3(b) bluehand/S,
142–3(bg) Binkski/S, 142–3(t) Gilmanshin/S, 142(bl) Arne
Bramsen/S, 142(br) artjazz/S, 142(br) Vasily Kovalev/S,
142(br) TrotzOlga/S, 142(cl) Cameron Davidson/CO, 142(cl) Ryan
Carter/S, 142(tr) Iakov Filimonov/S, 142(tr) GARY HINCKS/SPL,
143(bc) ARENA Creative/S, 143(bc) JULIE DERMANSKY/SPL,
143(br) alexsvirid/S, 143(cl) KPA/Zuma/Rex Features,
143(cr) Iourii Tcheka/S, 143(cr) Aaron Amat/S, 143(tr) Candice
Villarreal/US Navy/Handout/CO, 143(tr) stevemart/S,
145–6 c4dmodelshop.com, 145(bl) REED HOFFMANN/epa/CO,
145(br) Eric Nguyen/CO, 145(bl) Stephen Finn/S,
144(tr) Natykach Nataliia/S, 145(tl) GARY HINCKS/SPL,
146–7 Newspix/Rex Features, 146–7(bg) Claudio Divizia/S,
146(bl) CLAUS LUNAU/SPL, 147(br) DAVE HUNT/epa/CO,

147(tr) Lyndon Mechielsen/Newspix/RF, 148(bl) Zlatko Guzmic/S,
148(c) Atlaspix/S, 148(l) Elenamiv/S, 149(bc) Jim Stem/St.
Petersburg Times/WpN/PS, 149(bl) CURTIS COMPTON/AP/PA,
149(br) William McGinn/AP/PA, 149(tr) c.Warner Br/Everett/RF,
149(tr) Gangster/S

150 S.Borisov/S

All other photographs are from: Corel, digitalSTOCK, digitalvision,
Dreamstime.com, Fotolia.com, iStockphoto.com, John Foxx,
PhotoAlto, PhotoDisc, PhotoEssentials, PhotoPro, Stockbyte

Every effort has been made to acknowledge the source and
copyright holder of each picture. The publishers apologize for any
unintentional errors or omissions.